LITTLE BOOK OF
HMS
ARK ROYAL

Liam McCann

LITTLE BOOK OF
HMS
ARK ROYAL

First published in the UK in 2012

© Demand Media Limited 2012

www.demand-media.co.uk

Printed and bound in China

ISBN 978-1-909217-05-8

Contents

Introduction

Since its founding in the 16th century, the Royal Navy is considered the oldest branch of Britain's armed forces and is often called the 'Senior Service'. Before then, Britain relied on a few ships built around the time of Alfred the Great (871-899AD), which were then upgraded by future kings to protect the islands from Norse invaders. In the late 10th and early 11th centuries, King Ethelred the Unready realised the importance of having a fleet so he ordered an enormous number of ships to be built to fight the Danes.

In August 991 the Danish fleet arrived at Northey Island in Essex, and the two sides then fought a pitched land battle at Maldon. The English army was outnumbered and the Danes scored the first of several crushing defeats. They then extracted a monetary tribute from the natives under the pretence that it would protect the islanders from further attack, but the Danes immediately went back on their word and sent ships marauding up and down the Channel coast and into the Thames Estuary.

When King Sweyn launched yet another successful invasion in 1013,

RIGHT King Sweyn in 1013 as he became the first of the Danish Kings of England.

he decided to maintain a protective fleet via taxation, but this practice died out after the Norman Conquest and English naval power declined as a result. For the next two centuries the British fleet consisted solely of merchant ships that could be transformed into troop transports in times of war. The islands were well governed by subsequent monarchs and the threat from the continent declined, but, with hostilities renewing with the French at the beginning of the Hundred Years War in 1337, a navy became a priority once more.

King Edward III destroyed the French fleet at the Battle of Sluys in 1340, and the major battles of the conflict were then confined to French soil. The English fleet was expanded to supply troops in Normandy so that they

RIGHT Sir Walter
Raleigh

and the building of dedicated warships throughout the 15th century, a move that paid dividends during the reign of Elizabeth I and England's ongoing war with the Spanish.

A number of privateers accompanied the fledgling navy's marauders in hunting the treasure-laden Spanish galleons returning from South America. It was only a matter of time before the Spanish countered, which Philip II did in 1588 when he ordered the country's armada to destroy the British and Dutch fleets. The British had anticipated the Spanish retaliation, however, and they'd been preparing to repel a major offensive for more than two years.

In those days it was still customary for the crown to commandeer merchant ships and those in the hands of wealthy privateers. In 1586, Sir Walter Raleigh ordered a ship that, as was tradition, would bear the prefix 'Ark' and then the surname of the owner, thus Ark Raleigh. Plans for this galleon were submitted to the shipbuilder R. Chapman of Deptford and the 103-foot 800-ton ship was launched the following year. She was a formidable opponent with four 60-pound guns, four 30 pounders, twelve each of 18 pounders and

could continue operations against the old enemy. Some French raids did get through to England's ports on the south coast however, so the fleet was beefed up during the reign of Henry V.

Although the Hundred Years War officially ended in 1453, subsequent monarchs believed a strong navy would not only be useful in combat but also as a deterrent. Henry VIII appointed a secretariat to oversee the dockyards

9 pounders, six 6 pounders and 17 small-bore weapons spread across two gun decks, a double forecastle, a quarterdeck and a poop deck. She was also a useful troop transport with room for 100 soldiers among her complement of 268 sailors and 32 gunners.

Raleigh, of course, had his sights set on plundering the galleons crossing the Atlantic for personal gain but Elizabeth I, fearing reprisals from Philip, bought the ship just before her launch for £5,000 (which was simply deducted from Raleigh's tax bill). The ship was then handed over to her new commander, Lord High Admiral Charles Howard, First Earl of Nottingham, and renamed Ark Royal. The fleet at last had a flagship, and the name would live on for over four hundred years.

The defeat of the Spanish Armada boosted morale in Britain and gave the impression that the navy was indestructible by any foreign power. However, slaving raids by the Barbary Corsairs (pirates operating out of North Africa) in the early 17th century dispelled the myth and the navy had little success in countering their threat. Charles I gave the force a much-needed boost by building a fleet of small but powerful warships, but he could only pay for them by increasing taxes, a strategy that proved disastrous as it contributed to the outbreak of the English Civil War.

With Charles I having been executed and the monarchy abolished, Britain was seen as a soft target. Oliver Cromwell immediately expanded the navy to deter any Europeans thinking of invading and within a decade it was once again the most powerful in the world. Two sea wars were then fought against the Dutch, with both sides scoring victories, but, with the restoration of the monarchy under Charles II, the fleet was again laid up due to lack of funds.

The Dutch saw an opening in the English defences and ruthlessly exploited it, sailing up the River Medway

LEFT The defeat of the Spanish Armada, 8 August 1588.

to Chatham Docks in 1667 and burning the vast majority of the fleet at anchor. This was perhaps the most crushing defeat in the history of the navy. The English immediately joined forces with the French in a bid to counter this new

ABOVE Slaving raids by the Barbary Corsairs.

RIGHT A Dutch fishery after the Second Anglo-Dutch War.

threat but the Dutch were well drilled and they repelled every attack during the third Anglo-Dutch War (1672-74).

Under Chief Secretary to the Admiralty Samuel Pepys, the navy became more professional and better drilled. With greater power came greater responsibility and the fleet soon ended the threat from the Barbary Corsairs and forced the North African states to accept

favourable peace treaties with England. The navy's attention then turned back to France, and, in an alliance with the Dutch, the English scored victories that would see them dominate the waves for the next 100 years.

During the late 17th century the navy set aside government funds and started building dedicated warships. Crews were then recruited and trained to the highest standards of seamanship and combat. A class system based on officers of varying ranks and ordinary seamen was also established. This newly modernised navy, with its superior tactics and organisation, high standards of hygiene, extensive dockyard facilities, excellent logistical support and first-rate ship design, was the first professional military force in the world. When the Act of the Union united England and Scotland in 1707, the ships of both navies combined to form the Royal Navy of Great Britain.

For the next 200 years this navy was the largest and most powerful in the world, but when enemies joined forces it was still occasionally outnumbered. French marauders did score victories over the British and Dutch convoys in the Mediterranean but the Royal Naval

retaliation was emphatic and lasting: they destroyed the entire French fleet in the Mediterranean at the Battle of Toulon in 1707, and there were more victories over the Spanish when they tried to take the British-held territories of Gibraltar and Menorca.

Despite its size and superiority, the Royal Navy was expected to police trouble spots across the globe so it was often spread too thinly. It failed to break through the French blockade at the

Battle of Chesapeake in the American Revolutionary War so Britain could no longer support the colonial rebels. This led to their surrender at Yorktown, which effectively ended British involvement in North America.

When the introduction of lemons and other fresh vegetables finally eradicated scurvy in the late 18th century, British naval power was restored (the disease reportedly killed 130,000 of the 190,000 sailors conscripted during the Seven

BELOW The Battle of Trafalgar in 1805.

Years War with the French between 1755 and 1763). There can be no doubt that this advantage was rammed home by Horatio Nelson, one of the finest commanders in naval history. By this time, the British fleet numbered 600 cruisers, more than the rest of the world's navies combined.

A second engagement at Toulon in 1793 saw another enormous French fleet destroyed. The Spanish and Dutch promptly joined forces with the remains of the French navy but they too were routed at the Battle of Camperdown in 1797. Napoleon's army in Egypt was then left isolated after Nelson annihilated his fleet at the Battle of the Nile the following year. Britain proved her dominance by crushing a Danish force at the Battle of Copenhagen in 1801.

The Royal Navy's defining moment came at Trafalgar in 1805, however. Thirty-three British ships faced off against 41 ships of the French and Spanish navies off the southwest coast of Spain. Nelson shunned conventional naval tactics which dictated lining your fleet up opposite the enemy and then trying to pound them into submission. Instead, he divided his ships into two lines and drove them through the oppo-

sition at right angles in a manoeuvre known as crossing the T. It gave the French and Spanish an early advantage in that their ships could train all their portside guns at the Royal Navy but, as soon as their battle line had been crossed, Nelson opened up from both flanks and tore into the French fleet. They lost 22 ships and 14,000 men, while Nelson lost no ships and little more than 1,000 men. It was such a decisive engagement that it secured British naval supremacy until the middle of the 20th century.

Chapter 1

The Original Ark

The first incarnation of Ark Royal saw service immediately. In 1588, the Spanish Armada of 22 dedicated warships and 108 converted merchantmen under the command of the Duke of Medina Sidonia was dispatched to end English involvement in the Spanish Netherlands and decimate the number of privateers attacking the Spanish treasure galleons.

The fleet, boasting 8,000 sailors and 18,000 soldiers, was spotted off The Lizard in Cornwall on 19 July and a system of beacons was lit to convey the news along the south coast to the English fleet in Plymouth Harbour. The defending ships were trapped in port by the tide, however, and they had to tack upwind overnight before being able to engage the enemy two days later.

The Spanish fleet took up a defensive crescent while the English approached in two separate forces, Sir Francis Drake in Revenge on one wing and Lord Howard to the south in Ark Royal. The heavier Spanish warships were more adept at close-quarter combat so Drake and Howard peppered them with cannon fire from range to soften them up.

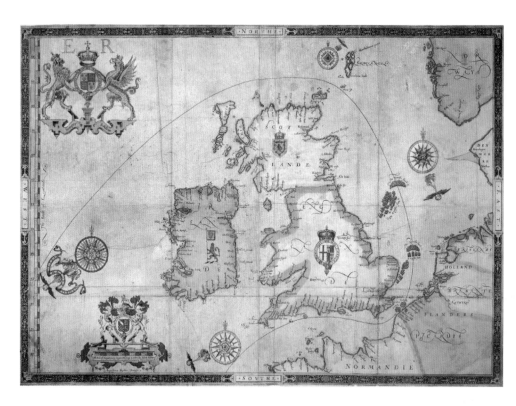

ABOVE The route around Britain that the Armada was forced to sail, based on Lord Howard's notes, 1590.

The range was too great, however, and only two Spanish ships were damaged when they collided in the confusion. Drake looted them that evening, capturing valuable gunpowder and gold.

Drake's greed almost proved costly because by daybreak the English fleet had become separated and the armada gained a day before the next engagement off Portland. It was not a significant battle and neither fleet lost any ships. The armada then ran for the safety of the Solent but the English launched a full-scale attack anyway. Just as a major naval action seemed inevitable, Medina Sidonia saw sense and ordered the Spanish to retreat into open water rather than beach on the treacherous sandbanks.

On 27 July, the armada reached Calais where they hoped to meet up with the Duke of Parma's 30,000-strong army that would oust Elizabeth from the English throne. It was then that things began to go wrong. The duke's army had been reduced to 16,000 by disease and they hadn't yet been equipped for the invasion. The barges that would transport them to the galleons had also been blockaded at Dunkirk by a fleet of 30 Dutch flyboats.

The English realised they had the Spanish trapped in a shallow anchorage and launched a fire-ship attack on the enemy fleet. Two of the eight ships were intercepted and towed away but the other six, laden with pitch, tar and gunpowder drifted amongst the armada. The Spanish ships had to cut their anchor cables and break ranks to escape the burning hulks and were then

ABOVE Sir Francis Drake.

forced into battle against the English fleet on their terms.

Medina Sidonia realised he was at a disadvantage and tried to form his ships into a defensive crescent off the small port of Gravelines in Flanders. The English surrounded them and closed to within a hundred yards to unload their heavy weapons at the Spanish.

The smaller English ships were more manoeuvrable and easily evaded the grappling lines while pouring shot into the enemy galleons. Sailors on the upper decks traded musket fire amidst the carnage.

By four o'clock in the afternoon, the English ships were running low on gunpowder and ammunition and they were forced to disengage. Five Spanish ships were lost outright and many others were severely damaged. Medina Sidonia took advantage of the southerly wind and headed north. Although low on ammunition and supplies, the English fleet gave chase so the armada couldn't stop to collect Parma's invasion force.

Ten days later, Lord Howard on Ark Royal called off the pursuit as the fleets approached the Firth of Forth. Medina Sidonia knew he couldn't return via the North Sea and the English Channel so he charted a course home around the north of Scotland.

The armada was then battered by severe storms for several weeks. With

RIGHT Duncannon Fort was built in 1588 in expectation of an attack by the Spanish Armada.

LEFT Rocky bay at Kinnagoe where the ship *La Trinidad Valencera* was wrecked in 1588.

supplies of food and water running low and with the sailors exhausted, the armada fought its final battle against the weather, and lost.

Around 50 ships were driven onto rocks in Ireland and Scotland and 5,000 men perished. Indeed only 67 ships and 10,000 men made it home, but many of them were to die from their wounds or from disease contracted on the voyage. It was an unmitigated disaster, although the weather had played the major part in defeating the invasion force.

It may have appeared that the engagement was an outright English victory and some of the statistics back this up: they lost no ships and only around 100 men during the series of engagements, but more than 6,000 men were discharged without pay afterwards and most died of hunger. Despite this appalling end to the battle, the English psyche received a tremendous boost and their naval superiority for the next 300 years can be traced back to the defeat of the armada.

The flagship Ark Royal survived the engagement and saw action again in a raid on the Spanish fleet in Cádiz eight years later. With Charles Howard at the helm and a large Dutch contingent backing the 150-strong fleet boasting 14,000 men, the British arrived in Cádiz Bay at the end of June.

The two sides engaged early on the morning of 30 June with an artillery barrage that resulted in four of the Spanish ships being lost. Anglo-Dutch forces then entered the inner bay and landed a company of men on the dock at El Puntal.

The Spanish were strangely disorganised and the invading army took the fort of San Felipe before the city itself surrendered. The British promptly sacked Cádiz and then tried to take control of the Spanish fleet that had retreated to Puerto Real. But the Duke of Medina

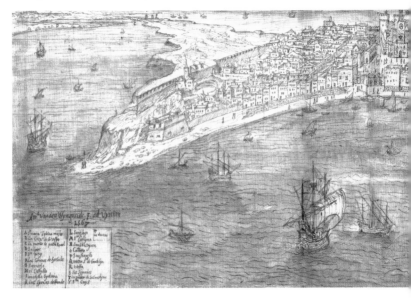

Sidonia ordered the fleet to be scuttled rather then let it fall into enemy hands so 32 galleys and treasure galleons were burned.

Although the Anglo-Dutch fleet lost 10 ships and 2,000 men, it was an extremely successful naval battle for them because it crippled the Spanish fleet, devastated the country's economy, destroyed an important port city and secured the release of hundreds of hostages. It also prevented the Spanish from launching anything other than a token invasion until 1599, when Ark Royal would once again be called into service as the flagship of the fleet. This time, however, Philip of Spain refused to dispatch a second armada and the war between the two countries was officially ended by King James I with the Treaty of London in 1604.

LEFT Cádiz Bay, 1567.

him marry his daughter, Maria Anna, so he returned to England and advised the Duke of Buckingham and King James to consider going back to war with Spain to recapture the glory days of the late Elizabethan period.

King James initially resisted but, when he died in March 1625, foreign policy was left in the hands of the new king, Charles I. War was immediately declared and plans were drawn up to decimate the treasure galleons and destroy the Spanish economy a second time by targeting Cádiz once more. Come the autumn, Charles had assembled a fleet of 105 ships under the Anne Royal and 15,000 men, but there was to be no repeat of the earlier success.

Ark Royal was immediately renamed Anne Royal after his consort, Anne of Denmark. Five years later she was given an extensive refit and converted into a full-rigged 42-gun battleship of the line. Although there followed 15 years of peace between the two nations, Prince Charles felt snubbed by the Spanish king's refusal to let

Storms weakened both men and machinery and, by the time the fleet eventually landed in Cádiz Bay, the crews were desperately malnourished. Sir Edward Cecil then made the fatal error of allowing his men to re-supply from the locals' wine stores. When the

Spanish army arrived they found the entire Anglo-Dutch crew drunk and promptly put 7,000 men to the sword without a shot being fired. The invading fleet also lost 62 ships in what was an unmitigated disaster.

The Anne Royal survived the encounter and remained in service until 1636 when she struck her own anchor in the River Medway while being transferred before becoming Sir John Pennington's flagship. The collision buckled her timbers and she sank in the river. She was raised at great cost but found to be damaged beyond repair and was finally broken up two years later. She would be the last ship christened Ark Royal for over three hundred years.

BELOW The River Medway where the original Ark, now renamed *Anne Royal*, sank.

Chapter 2

The Name Lives On

The second ship to bear the name Ark Royal wasn't initially intended for use by the Royal Navy but, with tension rising across Europe in the lead-up to the First World War, the government decided to buy a tramp steamer from the Blyth Shipbuilding Company in

BELOW *Ark Royal.*

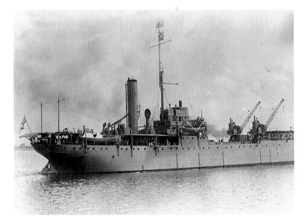

Northumberland – she would probably have ended up plying the coal and grain trade in the Black Sea – and convert her into a seaplane carrier. The admiralty had flirted with ships that carried aircraft before but it wasn't until they modified a cruiser in 1913 that the value of carrying seaplanes for aerial reconnaissance and anti-submarine patrols became apparent.

The unnamed tramp steamer had only just had her keel laid so there was plenty of scope to modify her plans and she was effectively the first ship in history to be purpose-built as a carrier. A large and open forward deck was required to recover the seaplanes and allow her few conventional aircraft to take off, so the main superstructure and single triple-expansion steam engine producing 3,000 horsepower had to be moved aft. This allowed the designers to incorpo-

ABOVE *Ark Royal* in 1914.

rate hangars, workshops and fuel stores in the centre of the ship beneath the forward deck. A pair of cranes on the bow lifted the aircraft from the hangar and could then recover them from the water's surface after their mission. She was unique in that her designers added a steadying sail to her mizzen mast, and she was eventually commissioned by the navy at the end of 1914.

She was designed to carry five Sopwith 807 seaplanes and four conventional, the latter having to return to a base on land because, on a ship only 366 feet long, there wasn't enough room to set down on the deck. The ship displaced 7,500 tons, cruised at 11 knots, had a range of 3,000 miles, was armed with four three-inch Armstrong-Whitworth 12-pound guns and was crewed by 60 aviation personnel and 120 officers and men.

The ship's 11-knot top speed meant she was too slow to work with the British fleet in the North Sea so she was dispatched to the Mediterranean to support the landings in the Dardanelles. She arrived on station late in February 1915 and immediately tried to launch her aircraft to reconnoitre the straits,

BELOW The Turkish ship, *The Goebe.*

but the first few missions were poorly organised and, although the Allies were shelling the Ottoman fortifications, the information from the aircraft wasn't seen as particularly important and yielded few results.

The aircrews soon learned to spot shipping mines but they were unable to prevent the loss of three British and one French ship in March. Although her aircraft also bombed the towns along the straits, the navy's 20-pound

weapons did little damage. Some success was achieved, however, when the aircrews spotted an ammunition dump and directed HMS Nelson's fire towards it in April. More success followed with Ark Royal's aircraft providing valuable support to the Australian and Kiwi forces at Anzac Cove on the Gallipoli peninsula but, when she began taking fire from Turkish ships and German U-boats, it seemed prudent to retreat to a safe haven at Imbros.

She remained in the port for six months before leaving for Salonika to provide support to British troops fighting the Bulgarians as well as conducting submarine patrols with her five Sopwith 166s and two seaplanes. The ship stayed in this theatre of operations for another year and a half before transferring again, this time to Mudros, to serve as a depot ship for all RNAS aircraft.

In January 1918 two Turkish ships, the Goeben and the battlecruiser Breslau, left the Dardanelles to attack the British fleet at Mudros. Two of Ark Royal's Sopwith Babies were scrambled to intercept but one was shot down and the other was forced to land with engine problems. The Breslau struck five mines and sank, while the Goeben struck two

and ran aground. Ark Royal's remaining aircraft tried to finish her off the next morning but their bombs missed and the single plane that had been modified to carry a torpedo couldn't take off with the extra weight.

In early April Ark Royal sailed for the island of Syros to support seaplanes of the RAF – which had been formed after the merger of the RNAS and the Royal Flying Corps – flying anti-submarine patrols. She then transferred to Piraeus, where she remained until the signing of the Armistice of Mudros at the end

LEFT New Zealand soldiers at Anzac Cove 1915.

of October. The ship then sailed for Constantinople to rejoin the rest of the Allied fleet.

Although the First World War had ended, there was still widespread conflict across the region and Ark Royal stayed in service to support White Russian forces against the Bolsheviks in the Black Sea. The ship was constantly on standby for the next two years, ferrying seaplanes to Malta in exchange for de Havilland bombers and personnel who would join the campaign against Mohammad Abdullah Hassan, the Mad Mullah, in Somalia. After his defeat and death in 1920, the ship was redirected to the Black Sea to assist struggling Russian forces, but she ended up transporting refugees out of the war zone. Having delivered a complement of men and machinery to Basra in the summer of 1920, she returned home for a refit.

She was soon re-commissioned and transported a dozen Bristol fighter aircraft back to the Dardanelles during the Chanak crisis in 1922. Turkish forces

RIGHT The Allied fleet enters the Dardanelles.

LEFT Satellite image of the Dardanelles.

had just defeated the Greeks at Smyrna and now threatened to attack the British and French guarding the neutral zone in the Dardanelles. The British issued a communiqué warning the Turks that war would be declared if they continued their advance, but the pro-Turkish French Prime Minister, Raymond Poincaré, had already ordered his troops to withdraw. Foreign Secretary Lord Curzon was dispatched to Paris to resolve the issue but an armistice with the Turks was only drawn up two hours before the British were due to attack.

David Lloyd George's premiership suffered during the crisis because the people of Britain were not ready to go back to war, and the countries of the Commonwealth protested that war could no longer be declared in their name without proper consultation. Canadian Premier Mackenzie King was the first to break ranks and insist that his parliament would decide his country's commitment and involvement with global affairs from that moment on. The other heads of state soon followed suit, leaving Britain isolated and in danger of losing control over her dominions.

Lloyd George reacted to the crisis by calling a meeting of the Conservative Party's MPs and stating his claim to fight the next general election as an independent party. This lost him the support of the post-war coalition and several cabinet ministers, including Lord Curzon, and MPs voted overwhelmingly to dissolve the alliance. Lloyd George was left with no option other than to resign from politics.

With war against the Turks having been avoided at the last moment, Ark Royal came home the following year. She was placed back on reserve as a depot ship for the navy's minesweepers in Sheerness for the next seven years. She was then fitted with a catapult to

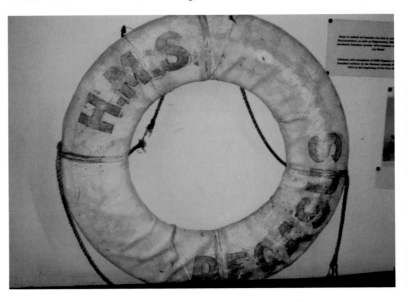

RIGHT Life bouy from *HMS Pegasus*.

launch her aircraft and used as a training ship throughout the 1930s.

In December 1934 she was renamed HMS Pegasus because the navy had commissioned a new aircraft carrier to lead the line, and, as was tradition, the flagship of the British fleet would be called Ark Royal. This is not the end of her story, however. She was used to train Swordfish, Seafox and Walrus pilots to use the catapult launching system before she was called upon to deliver a squadron of aircraft to Scapa Flow.

She was the nearest ship to the Royal Oak when the German submarine U-47 torpedoed the battleship in the anchorage in 1939 and she rescued 400 men from the water. Even so, more than 800 men went down with the ship or succumbed to their wounds in the next few days. The sinking caused outrage in Britain and its effect on the morale of the nation was considerable. Changes to dockside security were made immediately and anti-submarine defences were installed in every major port.

With her three Fairey Fulmar fighters, HMS Pegasus was then assigned to protect the Atlantic convoys from both the U-boat threat and aerial attacks from the Luftwaffe's Focke-Wulf 200 maritime patrol bombers. Although the Fulmars were launched from the Pegasus by catapult, they could not land on the short carrier deck. If they couldn't make land after their patrol, the pilots were faced with the unenviable task of deliberately ditching at sea and hoping to be rescued by a ship from the convoy.

THE NAME LIVES ON

RIGHT Oerlikon 20-millimetre cannon.

BELOW A Royal Navy *Supermarine Walrus* amphibian hanging from a crane aboard *HMS Pegasus*, September 1942.

The carrier escorted nine convoys from late 1940 through to July 1941. Her anti-aircraft defences were beefed up with a pair of Oerlikon 20-millimetre cannon on the bow, her bridge was enlarged and she was retrofitted with early-warning radar. The navy soon realised that the ship was well past her prime and decided to retire her for use as a training ship. She saw out the war as a barracks ship. By 1946, she was deemed too old for another refit and was scheduled for disposal.

She was saved at the last minute by R.C. Ellerman whose company planned to convert her to a freighter sailing under the Panamanian flag. Having been renamed Anita I, she was impounded by Ellerman's creditors and auctioned to a ship-breaker to pay off the debt. She was then sold once more – to the British Iron & Steel Corporation – before finally being broken up for scrap in Essex in 1950.

Chapter 3

Immediate Action

Designated pennant number 91, the third Ark Royal was ordered in 1934, had her keel laid down by Cammell Laird & Company the following year, was launched two years later and was finally commissioned in 1938, just a year before the outbreak of the Second World War. She would have been in service much earlier because her original plans were drawn up in the early 1920s but the economic downturn at the end of the decade saw the project shelved for five years.

By the time she had made it back to the drawing board there were several restrictions on the size and weight of ships because the world's naval powers were concerned about triggering an arms race as tension in Europe rose again. The treaties of Washington and London restricted tonnage on several classes of ship but they were due to expire in 1936. So Britain pushed for another treaty to limit the size of aircraft carriers to 22,000 tons to avoid a power struggle with Italy and Japan.

The second London Naval

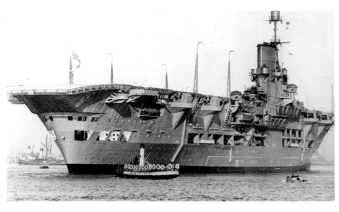

BELOW The third incarnation of the *Ark Royal* was an enormous aircraft carrier.

Treaty was signed by Britain, the United States and France in March 1936, but Italy and Japan refused to agree to its terms. This meant that some of the restrictions – on gun size for example – became obsolete immediately. Some of the tonnage limitations could also be circumvented if a country felt there was a threat to its national security from one of the nations that hadn't signed the agreement. The upshot was that aircraft carriers, for the time being at least, were actually limited to 23,000 tons.

The dry docks at Britain's bases in Malta and Gibraltar could only accommodate ships up to around 700 feet but Ark Royal's aircraft, even with steam-powered catapults to aid take-off and arrestors to aid landings, needed a flight deck 800 feet long. This meant the ship's designers had to lay a keel that would yield a waterline length of 721 feet, while the flight deck could be extended to overhang the ship's bow and stern. With two hangar decks for aircraft inside the hull, the flight deck needed to be more than 60 feet above the waterline, which eventually led to the now-familiar shape of all modern aircraft carriers.

Such was the height of the flight deck

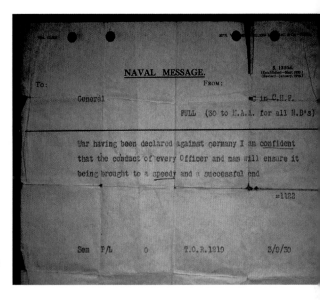

NAVAL MESSAGE.

To: General

FROM: C in C H.F.

FULL (30 to M.A.A. for all R.D's)

War having been declared against Germany I am confident that the conduct of every Officer and man will ensure it being brought to a speedy and a successful end

=1122

Sen P/L   O   T.O.R. 1819   3/9/39

ABOVE Declaration of war naval message received by the aircraft carrier *HMS Ark Royal*. The time of receipt was 18:19 on 03/09/1939.

and the superstructure that, to conform to the weight restrictions and ensure the ship remained stable in all weather conditions, only the engine room and magazines would be armour-plated: too much weight high above the waterline would have resulted in serious rolling in heavy seas. She was also strengthened with a four-inch armour belt around her waterline to protect against torpedo strikes.

The Royal Navy had learned much about the shortcomings of their capital ships and aircraft carriers in the First World War and they knew that speed was a major advantage, both in search-and-destroy missions and when fleeing from superior forces. Ark Royal's previous incarnation could only manage 11 knots and was therefore all but useless in tracking enemy battleships and cruisers. The new ship was fitted with six drum boilers powering three Parsons Turbines delivering 103,000 horsepower to her triple screws. On her sea

trials in May 1938 she managed 31 knots, which actually exceeded her design speed by a knot. She could cruise for 8,000 miles at 20 knots.

Her crew of 1,600 officers, sailors and airmen maintained a squadron of 50-60 Swordfishes, Skuas and Fulmars, and she was protected by 16 four-and-a-half-inch guns, 32 two-pounders and 32 anti-aircraft machineguns. On completion, she was the most expensive ship ever ordered by the Royal Navy. The £3,000,000 price tag equates to over £150 million in today's currency.

With the world once again on the brink of war it was inevitable that Ark Royal would see immediate service. German U-boats had already taken up positions in the Channel before the declaration of hostilities and they began sinking civilian and merchant ships within hours. Ark Royal was deployed as part of the home fleet's hunter-killer

ABOVE Skua Mk.II in flight.

group and saw action when responding to a distress call from the SS Fanad Head, which was being pursued by U-30. The carrier, under the command of Captain Arthur Power, launched her aircraft to intercept the U-boat but she was spotted and then fired upon by U-39.

Ark Royal immediately proved her worth by avoiding both torpedoes, and the carrier's escorts then depth-charged the submarine into submission. The Skuas arrived too late to save the Fanad Head, however, and two were lost in their own bomb blasts when they

RIGHT Winston Churchill.

dispatched to rescue the crippled submarine Spearfish. While returning to port, three Luftwaffe Dorniers spotted the carrier and her escorts, Rodney and Nelson, and attacked. Ark Royal launched her aircraft to intercept the German planes and shot one of them down immediately. The other two broke off their attack but it was clear that they would return with reinforcements now that the task group's position was known.

Three of the four Junkers 88 bombers that engaged the carrier were dispersed by its anti-aircraft batteries but one managed to drop a one-ton bomb. Ark Royal's speed

attacked the U-30 with a low-altitude pass. The admiralty were uneasy about the engagement and concluded that the near miss of the torpedoes, along with the successful U-boat attack on the aircraft carrier Courageous three days later, meant that carrier-led hunter-killer patrols were simply too risky.

Later the same month Ark Royal was

and manoeuvrability were again tested but she survived by turning hard-a-starboard and avoided the bomb by 30 metres. Most of the ship was covered in spray from the explosion so the German observers concluded that she must have been hit, and they then reported her sunk when a later reconnaissance flight only located the escorts.

The German propaganda machine went into overdrive with the news that the British flagship had been destroyed. Such was the concern in Britain and the Allied nations that the negative news would impact on morale that Winston Churchill personally reassured President Roosevelt the carrier was safely in port. When the news filtered back to Germany, it caused considerable embarrassment to the Nazi Party.

The following month Ark Royal was given the task of finding the German heavy cruiser Graf Spee, which was known to be patrolling the South Atlantic. She teamed up with the Renown and soon spotted the Graf Spee's refuelling tanker.

BELOW *HMS Ark Royal* photographed in 1939 with a Fairey "Swordfish" aircraft taking off as another approaches from astern.

They continued the chase towards South America and learned that the German cruiser had put into Montevideo to repair critical damage to her oil purification and desalination plants sustained during the Battle of the River Plate. Two Royal Navy cruisers had her trapped in the harbour but they would be hard pushed to prevent the much more powerful German ship escaping if Captain Hans Langsdorff decided to run for the open ocean.

RIGHT The German battleship Admiral *Graf Spee* in flames after being scuttled in the River Plate Estuary

BELOW The Admiral *Graf Spee*, a German pocket battleship.

So the British came up with a clever bluff to keep the Graf Spee in port: Ark Royal and Renown were still two days' sailing away but they had to convince Langsdorff they were lying in wait beyond the mouth of the harbour so they placed a bogus order for fuel from Buenos Aires, which was just five hours away. They made sure the order was leaked to Langsdorff and he, believing it would be better to save what he could from the ship before sinking her, rather than letting her fall into the hands of the British, decided to scuttle the Graf Spee in the Plate estuary. His decision was no doubt helped by the fact that the Uruguayan government was on good terms with the British. If the Graf Spee had been turned over to them, they would have allowed British intelligence officers operating in the city access to the ship.

Langsdorff had all the ship's vital components destroyed and then dispersed her remaining munitions throughout her holds. Forty men then sailed the ship into the estuary and blew the scuttling charges in front of a crowd of at least 20,000. Langsdorff and the skeleton crew were taken off by an Argentine tug and ferried back to the city, but the captain couldn't live with the guilt of losing his ship and shot himself three days later.

Having returned to Portsmouth for supplies, Ark Royal was then deployed in the Mediterranean for exercises that were cancelled a day later. She was instead transferred to Norway to assist British forces and provide fighter cover for the eight remaining ships in the task force. The German advance into Norway was overwhelming however, and no amount of air support could contain them. Ark Royal's aircraft therefore flew cover while Allied troops

RIGHT Funeral procession of Captain Hans Langsdorff, who shot himself on 20 December 1939.

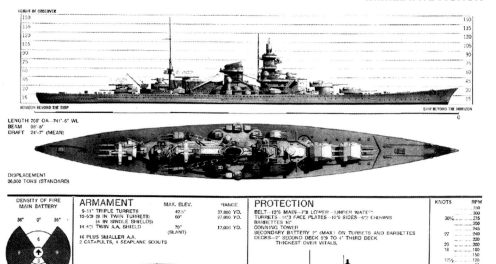

HEIGHT OF OBSERVER

150		150
135		135
120		120
105		105
90		90
75		75
60		60
45		45
30		30
15		15

HORIZON BEYOND THE SHIP   SHIP BEYOND THE HORIZON

LENGTH 700' OA—741'-6" WL.
BEAM   98'-5"
DRAFT   24'-7" (MEAN)

DISPLACEMENT
26,000 TONS (STANDARD)

DENSITY OF FIRE MAIN BATTERY	ARMAMENT	MAX. ELEV.	RANGE	PROTECTION	KNOTS	RPM

DENSITY OF FIRE
MAIN BATTERY

36°   0°   36°

6
9   9
3
145° 180° 145°

ARMAMENT

9–11" TRIPLE TURRETS   42.5°   37,000 YD.
12-5'9 (6 IN TWIN TURRETS)   60°   27,000 YD.
(4 IN SINGLE SHIELDS)
14-4'1 TWIN A.A. SHIELD   70°   17,000 YD.
                  (SLANT)
16 PLUS SMALLER A.A.
2 CATAPULTS, 4 SEAPLANE SCOUTS

PROTECTION

BELT—12"6 MAIN—7"8 LOWER—(UNDER WATER)
TURRETS—14"3 FACE PLATES—10"6 SIDES—6"2 CROWNS
BARBETTES 10"
CONNING TOWER
SECONDARY BATTERY 2" (MAX.) ON TURRETS AND BARBETTES
DECKS—3" SECOND DECK 5'9 TO 4" THIRD DECK
THICKEST OVER VITALS.

KNOTS	RPM
	350
	300
30½	275
	250
	245
27	240
	220
23	200
18	160
	150
12½	120
	80

DES. SPD   DES. HP
28 KTS   80,000

were evacuated. During the three-day operation the ship was repeatedly attacked by the Luftwaffe but no direct hits were recorded and she made it safely back to Scapa Flow.

Captain Power was immediately promoted to the admiralty so Ark Royal took on a new commander, Captain Cedric Holland. His first task was to complete the withdrawal from Norway but this time the operation didn't go as smoothly.

Three ships from the task force were sunk by the German battleships Scharnhorst and Gneisenau but Ark Royal's aircraft couldn't find them and they escaped. As the evacuation wound down, however, Scharnhorst was spotted in Trondheim and attacked, disastrously. Eight of Ark Royal's 15 Skuas were shot down and two British destroyers, HMS Electra and HMS Antelope, collided in fog, while the German battleship escaped damage.

ABOVE Recognition drawing of the *Scharnhorst,* prepared for intelligence purposes, depicting the ship as refitted in 1939.

The carrier returned to Scapa Flow and was immediately reassigned to the Mediterranean with the battlecruiser HMS Hood and three escort destroyers. Once there, the admiralty faced a tough decision because the French had capitulated and there was a danger their fleet would fall into enemy hands. Cedric Holland was the man sent to negotiate an outcome favourable to the British, which meant surrendering to Ark Royal or scuttling the fleet before the Axis Powers got their hands on the ships. To Holland's dismay, the French Admiral François Darlan refused to surrender the fleet so Churchill took what must have been one of his darkest and most uncomfortable decisions of the entire war: he chose to sink the French fleet at anchor off the Algerian coast at Mers-el-Kébir.

The battleship Bretagne was sunk and five other ships were seriously damaged, although the Strasbourg did escape. Allied losses were tiny, however: just two men and six aircraft. The attack damaged relations between the Allies and France because it resulted in the deaths of nearly 1,300 French servicemen and wounded another 350, but, had the fleet been captured by the Germans, it might have inflicted severe casualties on the Atlantic convoys and the escorts protecting

RIGHT Map of Scapa Flow and surrounding area.

them. We'll never know.

Ark Royal was then instructed to help protect Malta from an increasing number of Italian air force raids, and it then dispatched its own aircraft to inflict severe damage on the Italian air base at Cagliari. After a couple more low-key operations, the ship came home for a refit in October. She then returned to Gibraltar to escort supply convoys to Malta and Alexandria, with one such run involving a skirmish with the Italian navy. It was the first of many operations against the Italians which continued with air attacks on Genoa and the oil refinery at La Spezia.

An action with a far greater long-term significance involved Ark Royal's half-sister HMS Illustrious. A daring plan was hatched to destroy the Italian fleet at anchor in the port of Taranto using torpedo bombers from the carrier. On the night of 11

November 1940, 21 Swordfishes were launched from the carrier to attack the port. The assault was perfectly timed and well executed. Three battleships – half of the fleet's capital ships – were sunk or permanently disabled.

ABOVE *Ark Royal's* half-sister *HMS Illustrious.*

RIGHT Erwin Rommel.

favour of the Allies.

But the action had far-reaching consequences that wouldn't be fully understood for another year: the Japanese took a keen interest in the tactic of using torpedo bombers to decimate a poorly protected fleet at anchor and revived it with devastating effect on 7 December 1941, when they attacked Pearl Harbour.

With the Scharnhorst and Gneisenau having been ordered back into the Atlantic to disrupt the Allied war effort, the admiralty made the decision to dispatch Ark Royal and her task force to find and sink the German raiders. In March 1941, aircraft from the carrier forced three German ships to surrender but they only caught up with the Scharnhorst at the end of the month. It looked like Ark Royal was in position to dispatch her torpedo bombers and attack the great battleship when a catapult malfunctioned and destroyed one of her Swordfishes. The remains of the aircraft were flung

Four merchantmen and a torpedo boat were then destroyed by the British task force. The balance of power in the Mediterranean had swung firmly in

into Ark Royal's path and she was then damaged when the bomber's depth charges exploded. She was forced back to Gibraltar to make repairs while the German battleships reached the safety of Brest on the French Atlantic coast.

By May, Erwin Rommel's Afrika Corps were pushing the Western Desert Force to the brink of collapse and were about to capture strategic locations along the North African coast. The decision was made to send reinforce-

ments by task force from Gibraltar to Alexandria. Now under the command of Captain Loben Maund, Ark Royal led the enormous flotilla of transport ships, destroyers, cruisers and a battleship into the danger zone.

They were immediately spotted by the Italian air force, which then alerted the Luftwaffe. Twelve of Ark Royal's Fairey Fulmars put up a spirited defence and saw off over 50 enemy aircraft, but only seven were left by the time a second

LEFT *Ark Royal* with a flight of "Swordfish" overhead.

RIGHT Map of the Operation "Rheinübung" and Royal Navy operations against the batttleship *Bismarck,* with approximate movements of ship groups and places of aerial attacks

wave of 34 German aircraft attacked at dusk. The other ships in the convoy opened up with a withering hail of anti-aircraft fire and also repelled this attack, however. The large proportion of the convoy reached Alexandria without further incident but another crisis was already brewing in the North Atlantic.

The mighty German battleship Bismarck and heavy cruiser Prinz Eugen had broken through the Allied blockade (as part of Operation Rheinübung) to wreak havoc on the Atlantic convoys ferrying supplies to Britain. At over 820 feet long and displacing more than 53,000 tons fully loaded, the Bismarck,

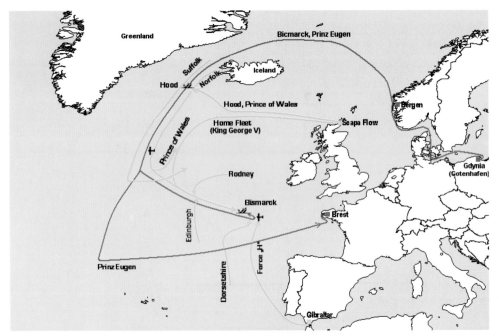

LEFT British battlecruiser *HMS Hood.*

with her eight 15-inch guns, which were capable of firing a projectile the size of a small car more than 20 miles, and 56 smaller anti-aircraft batteries, was the pride of Hitler's fleet and one of the most powerful battleships afloat.

Although the mission was supposed to be a secret, a Spitfire reconnaissance plane spotted the two ships leaving the Norwegian fjord. The navy was therefore on high alert by the time the Bismarck and Prinz Eugen reached the North Sea. The German ships headed north towards Iceland, however, to

avoid the Royal Navy and make their attack through the Denmark Strait. But the British had anticipated their course and sent ships to patrol the sea between Iceland and Greenland. The Suffolk and Norfolk soon spotted the German battleships and gave chase but Bismarck warned them off by rapid-firing her main batteries. Instead of inflicting damage on the British, however, the Bismarck's gun blast only damaged her own radar.

Once in the Denmark Strait the German ships were engaged by the

British battlecruiser HMS Hood and the battleship Prince of Wales. But Hood, the pride of the British navy, made a fatal mistake and targeted the Prinz Eugen rather than the Bismarck. The mighty German battleship was equipped with more sophisticated aiming equipment and immediately sighted on the Hood, her first two salvos promptly straddling the British battlecruiser.

Admiral Holland on the Hood's bridge decided to close the gap between the ships, firstly to negate the German advantage and secondly because long-range fire would fall steeply on the ship and her deck armour was relatively thin. But Bismarck reacted quickly and

turned to starboard to stay at optimum firing range. Her next salvo admitted the coup de grace: a single shell penetrated Hood's aft magazine and her 15-inch shells detonated sympathetically.

The Prince of Wales also suffered heavy damage during the exchange, although a shell from her forward turret penetrated the Bismarck's deck and blew a large exit hole through a fuel tank. This was to prove crucial in the coming battle as it meant Bismarck only had enough fuel left to reach northern France, which would mean safety under the protection of the Luftwaffe.

The loss of the Hood was another heavy blow to morale at home.

RIGHT Looking aft at *HMS Hood's* 15″ guns

BELOW *The Bismarck*

Only three sailors survived the massive explosion and sinking. Fearing the Atlantic convoys would be no match for such fearsome opponents, Churchill gave Captain Maund on Ark Royal one of the most famous orders of the war: Sink the Bismarck!

Despite committing more than a dozen large ships and at least 30 smaller vessels to the chase, the Bismarck and Prinz Eugen eluded the British fleet for another week, but the former was finally found by Swordfish reconnais-sance aircraft from Ark Royal at the end of May. The fleet was too far behind however, and the only way to prevent the Bismarck from reaching the relative safety of the French port at Saint-Nazaire was to dispatch a flight of Swordfishes to engage and disable her. A first wave of aircraft confused the British cruiser HMS Sheffield with the German ship and fired on her by mistake. Thankfully the torpedoes were fitted with unreliable detonators and most exploded when they hit the water.

RIGHT *HMS Sheffield.*

Having signalled their apology, the Swordfish bombers returned to Ark Royal to take on more fuel.

Now armed with torpedoes that would only explode on contact with the ship's hull, the 15 Swordfish bombers were launched again at just after seven in the evening, and they finally engaged the Bismarck at sunset. Under intense bombardment from the gun crews on deck, which included the Bismarck's main batteries firing into the water to try downing the aircraft with the impact spray, the Swordfishes made their passes and dropped their torpedoes, although only three struck the ship, two forward of the engine rooms and one, launched by either John 'Jock' Moffat or Kenneth Pattisson, jamming the rudder.

Unable to steer, the Bismarck was now exactly where the British wanted her, although she was by no means helpless and continued pounding the Sheffield from long range. Just after nine o'clock that evening, operational commander Admiral Günther Lütjens reported that the ship was unable to manoeuvre and, unless the rudder could be repaired, she would make her final stand by fighting to the last shell the following morning.

During the night the Bismarck was

ABOVE *Bismarck's* Captain Ernst Lindemann.

repeatedly attacked by British destroyers but there was little damage inflicted on either side. Come the morning, the battleships King George V and the Rodney, as well as a number of cruisers, opened up from around 20,000 yards and began pounding the Bismarck.

Unable to steer or accelerate to more than about seven knots, and with an increasing list aboard ship, the Bismarck's gunners found it almost impossible to return fire. Under ferocious bombardment and tens of direct hits, her remaining guns then fell silent, but her hull was sound and her engines were still running. The British fleet moved to within two miles and emptied their magazines at the crippled battleship but still she refused to go down.

Having fired over 700 main battery shells, the British were now low on ammunition and fuel, so Admiral John Tovey withdrew the Rodney, the King George V and the destroyers, and left the Dorsetshire to finish the German battleship with her torpedoes. One or two of the warheads may have hit but by now the German sailors knew the ship was lost and set scuttling charges. Bismarck finally sank just before eleven in the morning, some 2,000 sailors making it into the water before she went down.

Just after nine o'clock, a 16-inch shell from the Rodney struck the Bismarck's forward superstructure. The explosion killed hundreds of men, probably including Captain Ernst Lindemann and Lütjens, and almost knocked the two bow turrets out of action. Half an hour later, all of the German ship's main batteries had been silenced.

The remaining British ships moved in to rescue the survivors but U-boats had apparently been spotted in the area and the rescue attempt was aborted. Only 110 sailors were picked up by the British and five more were rescued by the U-74 the following day. It was a bitter blow to the Kriegsmarine, and the loss of their finest battleship was felt across Germany. The engagement proved that the days of the great battleships were numbered. Air power from Ark Royal had demonstrated that it was possible to find and sink the largest warships relatively easily and cheaply, in terms of men and equipment.

LEFT Admiral Somerville visits *Ark Royal* to congratulate the ship's company after the successful engagement with the *Bismarck*, October 1941.

The war in the Mediterranean was not going as well, however. Rommel was preparing to move into Egypt and Greece had already fallen to the Axis. Malta became even more important as a result and the island needed a constant supply of aircraft, equipment and personnel under increasing Italian attack. Ark Royal was again pressed into service but trouble was on the horizon.

As Rommel was also losing supplies to British raiders, Hitler decided to send more U-boats to the Mediterranean to counter the threat. While returning to Gibraltar to collect supplies, the two sides finally met and this time Ark Royal was the victim of a torpedo strike. The U-81 fired four torpedoes, one of which struck amidships on her starboard side and ripped a huge hole in her hull over a hundred feet long. The starboard boiler rooms, switchboard, oil tanks and bilge were immediately flooded and half the ship lost power. To make matters worse, shipboard communications then failed. Amazingly, only one crew-

RIGHT A *U-boat's* battery room with a torpedo is displayed at the Deutsches Museum in Munich, Germany.

man, Able Seaman Edward Mitchell, was killed in the initial explosion.

Captain Maund ordered her to stop but in just a quarter of an hour she was listing by 18 degrees. Britain had already lost two aircraft carriers, Courageous and Glorious, both of which sank quickly, so time was of the essence if the ship's company were going to be saved. Maund instructed everyone to assemble on the flight deck before giving the order to abandon ship. Thankfully one of the escort ships, HMS Legion, was able to draw alongside and save nearly 1,500 men.

And although several attempts were made to restart her boilers and her pumps, these ultimately proved unsuccessful. When the list reached 27 degrees in the early hours of the following morning, the salvage teams were also ordered to abandon ship. Just after six o'clock, Ark Royal rolled over, broke apart and sank.

RIGHT Another
view of *HMS Legion*
rescuing *Ark Royal's*
crew.

BELOW *HMS Legion*,
was able to save
nearly 1,500 men.

Despite saving everyone on the ship, a Board of Inquiry established immediately after the sinking blamed Captain Maund for a series of poor decisions and court-martialled him. He was found guilty of negligence on two counts: failing to send damage control parties to assess the impact and deal with the consequences, and failing to ensure the ship was prepared for such an eventuality.

A second committee also concluded that there were several design flaws in the ship itself: she could have been fitted with back-up diesel generators in case her primary power sources were compromised, because then her pumps and lights would have remained operational for longer; and several bulkheads were to be repositioned on future carriers to prevent widespread flooding from compartment to compartment. The inquiry's last statement suggested that the ship sank a little more than 20 miles east of the southern tip of Gibraltar.

This was not the end of her story, however. Several attempts had been made to find the wreck but all were unsuccessful until the BBC launched another expedition in 2002. Using autonomous underwater vehicles (AUVs) and advanced high-resolution side-scan sonar equipment, they finally found the ship 35 miles east of Gibraltar in 3,500 feet of water. The hull had broken apart and there was a large debris field surrounding the two sections.

Chapter 4

The 'Mighty Ark'

An order was placed for a replacement flagship immediately and the fourth Ark Royal's keel was laid down in early May 1943. Four Audacious-class aircraft carriers were initially ordered but two, HMS Africa and HMS Eagle, were seen as superflu-

BELOW The Royal Navy aircraft carrier *HMS Ark Royal* (R09).

ous to requirements at the end of the Second World War and cancelled. With no pressing need to get the other two ships into service, Audacious (which was soon renamed Eagle) and Ark Royal were redesigned for peace-keeping in the post-war years.

She was finally launched from the Cammell Laird shipyard seven years later but outfitting took another five years. During this time both she and her sister underwent several design changes so they were markedly different when commissioned in February 1955. Ark Royal was the first carrier to have an angled flight deck, was 804 feet long and, by the time she was decommissioned in 1978, displaced 54,000 tons.

She was powered by eight three-drum boilers delivering more than 150,000 horsepower through four sets of Parson Turbines to four prop shafts. Her top speed was 32 knots, and she could cruise at 14 knots for 7,000 nautical miles. She carried 2,640 officers, seamen and aircrew, and up to 50 aircraft, which were usually Sea Hawks, Skyraiders and Gannets. She was also heavily defended with 16 four-and-a-half-inch guns and 52 anti-aircraft cannons.

Her two steam catapults were capable of launching aircraft weighing up to 14 tons, and the design of her flight deck allowed aircraft to land and take off at the same time. After a refit in the late 1960s she was capable of handling larger jets like the Buccaneer and Phantom.

Unlike her predecessors, this incarnation of Ark Royal saw no active combat service, although she did partake in numerous fleet operations and NATO exercises throughout the Cold War. (She was scheduled to be deployed during the Suez Crisis in 1956 but she was still undergoing sea trials.) In 1963 she was used to trial the new vertical take-off and landing aircraft that would eventually see service during the Falklands War as the Hawker Harrier.

In 1965 the ship was sent to Rhodesia after the white minority declared the country's independence from Britain. The United Nations Security Council imposed sanctions, which Britain saw as legal justification for implementing a blockade and an oil embargo, although they stopped short of sending in an invading force.

ABOVE A lifebelt from *HMS Ark Royal* is displayed at the Williamson Art Gallery and Museum in Merseyside, England.

The Beira Patrol, as it was known, stayed in the area until 1975, with ships of all classes being rotated to maintain pressure on the Rhodesians. With defence cuts biting and the Rhodesians rationing the valuable oil, Prime Minister Edward Heath eventually called off the blockade, which had cost more than £100 million.

While patrolling the Eastern Mediterranean between Malta and Crete in 1970, Ark Royal collided with the Russian destroyer that was shad-

owing her. Both ships only sustained minor damage, although several of the destroyer's crewmen were forced into the water and two were never recovered. The incident should never have happened because Ark Royal was conducting night flying exercises and displaying the correct lighting configuration for a ship that could not manoeuvre.

No sooner had she launched her first aircraft than the Soviet ship approached on a collision course and, despite a desperate attempt to run the British

RIGHT *HMS Ark Royal* (R09).

ABOVE An overhead view of the Royal Navy aircraft carrier *HMS Ark Royal (R09)*, taken from an aircraft from the U.S. Navy carrier *USS Independence (CVA-62)*.

flagship hard astern and avoid the impact, the destroyer's port quarter struck Ark Royal's port bow. The Board of Inquiry set up to investigate the collision concluded that, although the Cold War practice of shadowing enemy ships was normal, Ark Royal was blameless in this instance and the practice of playing cat-and-mouse should be avoided whenever possible. Captain Ray Lygo was subsequently exonerated at his court-martial and returned to active service immediately.

The ship was then dispatched to British Honduras in Central America to deter an invasion by Guatemala as the British colony was granted independence. Its Buccaneers flew several

FAR RIGHT An aerial view of *HMS Ark Royal* alongside the U.S. nuclear-powered aircraft carrier *USS Nimitz* at Norfolk Naval Station, Virginia (USA), 1978. *Ark Royal* was decommissioned shortly afterwards.

RIGHT A Harrier performing a vertical take-off

Northwest Atlantic. She then returned to Fort Lauderdale in 1978 before coming home to the Royal Naval Station at Devonport for decommissioning the following year.

Her 29-year career involved no combat duty but she was used as a deterrent and to enforce the Rhodesian blockade, and during this time the 'Mighty Ark' became a household name. She was towed to Stranraer in Scotland and broken up for scrap over the next three years, although some parts survive, like her anchor, which serves as a memorial at the Fleet Air Arm Museum in Yeovilton. Her scrapping marked the end of all fixed-wing aircraft on British ships, the navy preferring to use helicopters and vertical take-off Harriers on HMS Hermes and the remaining Invincible-class carriers. However, one of the two Queen Elizabeth-class carriers due for entry into service in 2016 will almost certainly be configured to maintain a variant of the fixed-wing multi-role F-35 ground attack stealth fighter.

missions over the territory as a show of force and the invasion never took place.

In 1976 the ship represented British forces at the American bicentennial celebrations at Fort Lauderdale, Florida. On her return, she was featured in a BBC documentary called Sailor, which followed life aboard ship during a six-month training operation in the

Chapter 5

The End of an Era

With the previous flagship about to be scrapped, public pressure forced the navy to change the name of her replacement, the Indomitable, to Ark Royal so that the tradition lived on. The latest ship to bear the famous name was ordered in 1978 as the third ship –

BELOW The last *HMS Ark Royal* under construction in March 1981.

after her sisters Illustrious and Invincible – in the class. Her keel was laid down by Swan Hunters at Wallsend, Tyne and Wear, that December. She was launched by her sponsor, Queen Elizabeth, the Queen Mother, in June 1981 but wasn't commissioned for another four years. (The ship was apparently offered to the Australian navy but the Royal Navy relented and eventually offered them HMS Invincible instead.)

At only 689 feet in length and weighing 22,000 tons, she was considerably smaller than her predecessors (although larger than the other two ships in her class due to late modifications). She had four Rolls-Royce Olympus gas turbines delivering nearly 100,000 shaft horsepower, a top speed of more than 30 knots and a range of over 9,000 nautical miles. And with a complement of more than 1,000 men – of whom

366 were airmen – up to 18 Harriers and 10 Sea King or Merlin helicopters, three Phalanx and two 20mm guns for defence, the ship still packed a heavy punch. When required, the ship also hosted up to 400 Royal Marines for immediate deployment into a war zone.

The ship didn't see service during the Falklands War in 1982 but she was eventually dispatched from Portsmouth to patrol the North Atlantic for Russian submarines in 1985. She then headed to the Adriatic in the Mediterranean to support fleet operations during the Bosnian War in 1993. Under Captain Terry Laughran, the ship oversaw the humanitarian effort of the 2,400 British service personnel in the region.

RIGHT Example of
Sea Dart missiles.

BELOW A Royal
Navy BAe Sea Harrier
FA2 launching from
the flight deck.

Her aircraft were on standby in case the people on the ground were in need of combat air support, while her helicopters were well-equipped to deal with a mass withdrawal if the situation deteriorated. The task group itself was supposed to deprive the Serbs of valuable fuel and weapons for their ethnic cleansing programme but some hardware clearly made it through.

The following year Nick Richardson's Sea Harrier was lost to a surface-to-air missile over Gorazde during heavy fighting between the Serbs and Bosnian Muslims. His was the first British jet to be lost since the Falklands so concerns were raised about the flagship's mission. Thankfully, Lieutenant Richardson escaped to Bosnian lines and was rescued by an SAS team.

At the end of the war, Ark Royal was sent home and was given a minor refit between 1999 and 2001 (which saw her Sea Dart missile defences removed) but she was called into service again in 2003. After the first Gulf War, and through-

out the remainder of the 1990s, tension had been rising in the gulf states of the Middle East. With the disarmament of Saddam Hussein's forces in 1991 came the discovery that he had been stockpiling biological and chemical weapons, programmes that had begun with the help of the United States and Britain in the early 1970s. Instead of removing Saddam, however, the West decided upon a policy of monitoring and containment using economic sanctions and no-fly zones.

Following the expulsion of United Nations weapons inspectors in 1997, and a growing fear that Saddam was rebooting his weapons programmes, which involved possible nuclear capability, the US rushed through official foreign policy that had the express intent of removing Saddam from power. George W. Bush only added to the pressure on the Iraqi leader by insisting on carrying out the Iraqi Liberation Act. All that was needed was a catalyst to spark the invasion, and that occurred

RIGHT Tony Blair and George W. Bush wrap up a news conference at Camp David in March 2003.

on 11 September 2001, with the attacks on New York and Washington.

Despite UN Resolution 1441 not formally giving permission for US and British forces to go into Iraq, the Bush administration convinced Tony Blair to commit British personnel to the invasion, which was then officially (a number of Special Force operations had been going on for at least a year) launched on 19 March 2003. Nearly 150,000 US service personnel were joined by 45,000 British, 2,000 Australian and a handful of Polish troops.

Ark Royal was the first of 15 British ships to reach the area. She joined the US 5th Fleet and spearheaded a powerful task force comprising 5,000 naval personnel and 3,000 Royal Marine commandos.

THE END OF AN ERA

RIGHT A satellite shot of Iceland's Eyjafjallajökull volcano in 2010.

BELOW *HMS Ocean* at the 2005 International Fleet Review.

The ship was only equipped with helicopters during the war instead of her usual complement of Harriers. Her only losses occurred when two of her Sea Kings collided, claiming six British and one American life.

The flagship returned to the UK for another refit in 2004 because her sister, Illustrious, was already back in service. And she was again in Portsmouth for upgrades in 2006-07 before she returned to the fleet under new commander, Captain John Clink. She was required for civilian duty almost immediately when Prime Minister Gordon Brown dispatched her to France to rescue travellers stranded by the eruption of the Eyjafjallajökull volcano in Iceland. She accompanied the helicopter carrier HMS Ocean as part of Operation Cunningham.

Sadly, the Mighty Ark's days were numbered. While she was in Halifax, Nova Scotia, taking part in Canadian bicentennial celebrations, Prime Minister David Cameron announced that the ship would be decommissioned as the defence budget was cut by eight percent. Her replacement would be the HMS Prince of Wales, one of the new Queen Elizabeth-class aircraft carriers. In December 2010, the amphibious warfare ship HMS Albion succeeded Ark Royal as the flagship of the British fleet and it appeared that the four-hundred-year-old naval tradition had been broken.

Chapter 6

The Final Voyage

BELOW Well-wishers wave from the Round Towers in Portsmouth.

Two hours before sailing from Portsmouth on what would become her final voyage, Warrant Officer Simon Cox lined the junior men along Ark Royal's flanks to bid the city goodbye in

BELOW Well-wishers wave from the Round Towers in Portsmouth.

a formation known as Procedure Alpha. The tradition of having the ship's company visible as they leave port dates back to Nelson's era and was designed to show onlookers that the ship had peaceful intentions as her crew and defences were all visible. But it doubled as a non-hostile show of force too, as everyone who worked aboard exuded strength.

While the navy band played, Ark Royal's two tugs nudged her into the main channel through the harbour. Manoeuvring into the Solent requires great skill as shifting sands on the sea-floor meant Ark Royal only had three metres of clearance before she reached open water. As the ship passed the round towers and hundreds of well-wishers, the crew were allowed to wave their goodbyes – they wouldn't be back for another five months.

When Ark Royal was 10 miles offshore, her aircraft began arriving. Lynx, Sea King and Merlin helicopters were first onboard. Then, under the guidance of Flight Lieutenant Chris Pearson, came the Harriers of the naval strike wing. As they were also decommissioned in the defence cuts, this was the last time they would be deployed on the navy's flagship.

When the ship had all her aircraft onboard, she headed for Scotland to meet her task group for an operation called Joint Warrior. Along with ships from other NATO countries, Ark Royal's mission was to show how prepared she was to defend herself when she came under attack from a hostile force.

In the operations room, the ship was being made ready to deal with the opening strikes in the exercise. When all the crew were at their actions stations, the ship is said to be in State One, Condition Zulu, and it is now ready to go to war. The crew then ran through a series of drills to make certain they were ready for any eventuality,

ABOVE Aircraft begin arriving.

including adopting the brace position in case of a missile strike.

Having met up with the rest of the Auriga Task Group, Ark Royal headed for Canada. During the North Atlantic crossing, her Harriers were put through their paces to assess their readiness for action.

The aircraft took off using the ski jump to save fuel but they landed vertically on the deck in designated spots that were reinforced to cope with the enormous pressure of the downdraft from the Harrier's jet nozzles. The pilots had to complete a series of night landings before they were fully qualified. This is extremely difficult on a ship underway as there are few reference points or a horizon to help the pilot position the aircraft.

RIGHT & BELOW
The ski jump is used to save fuel.

With her final posting going according to schedule, the meteorology team suddenly realised that the Eyjafjallajökull volcano in southern Iceland was erupting. It was sending a plume of ash across the North Atlantic towards Scotland. A British Airways jet flew through an ash cloud at night in 1982, the fine shards of rock clogging the engines and causing the aircraft to fall five miles. Thankfully Captain Moody managed to get the plane on the ground safely but, since then, aircraft are forbidden from flying through volcanic ash.

As a result of the eruption, most major airports across Northern Europe were shut down, stranding thousands of passengers.

Second-in-Command of Ark Royal, Executive Officer Rob Bellfield, took the decision to ground all the ship's aircraft. With a weather front moving in that could bring corrosive sulphuric acid rain, Bellfield was then forced to secure all Ark Royal's aircraft below-decks. With the decks clear, physical training instructor Steve Losh took the

opportunity to put the crew through their paces with a series of sprints and fitness exercises.

Things quickly turned more serious however, when it was discovered that the ship's bilge had sprung a leak in the engine room. The crew quickly built a wooden box to fit around the pipe and packed it with quick-drying cement to fashion a temporary repair. Six hours later the cement had cured and the repair was effective.

The ship had now cleared the volcanic

RIGHT The sun rises after a night-flying training exercise.

ash so the pilots could resume their night-flying training. Flight Lieutenant Chris Pearson had to complete landings from just after dusk until the dead of night to earn his qualifications but, just when it seemed he'd pass this final test, the ash cloud spread further across Northern Europe and the ship's aircraft were grounded again.

This freed Ark Royal to return to Portsmouth to coordinate the rescue operation for the Britons stranded abroad. Captain Clink and XO Bellfield decided that they could carry up to 2,000 people if required, although it was a logistical nightmare working out how and where to house them on a ship that was never designed as a liner. One of the ship's hangars was hastily turned into a passenger compartment. Three hundred children's lifejackets, several tons of extra food and water, and a number of chairs and tables were taken onboard to make the civilians comfortable on their voyage home.

To save time in port, Ark Royal was refuelled at sea by her support ship RFA Victoria. This delicate operation required the support ship to pull alongside and transfer fuel through hoses into Ark Royal's tanks. As soon as she was refuelled, the weather centre reported that the ash cloud was lifting so Ark Royal stood down from Operation Cunningham.

ABOVE The crew line up for Procedure Alpha as the ship leaves Portsmouth.

THE FINAL VOYAGE

As she was about to return to the task group, a second leak was discovered below-decks. The sea chest, a small tank used to cool the engines, was leaking salt water into Ark Royal's fuel supply. Captain Clink decided not to rejoin the task group and to return instead to Portsmouth to make repairs. Divers were sent down to inspect the 25-year-old hull. They found that a crack had breached one of the fuel tanks and allowed salt water in to mix with the fuel. The problem was so serious that the fuel tanks would have to be drained before a welding crew would be allowed in to repair the damage. This meant the ship would have to go into dry-dock so Clink gave most of the crew a long weekend off.

The unscheduled stop allowed a group of cadets to familiarise themselves with the ship in case they were needed for the remainder of the voyage. They then faced a 30-minute exam to test their knowledge of the ship, the results of which determined whether they were fit to serve onboard. They were eventually summoned to the quarterdeck to find out if they had achieved the 80% pass mark.

Ark Royal fit snugly into the dock under the guidance of Chief Harbour Pilot Tony Bannister and the ship's Second Navigational Officer, Lieutenant Matt Duce. Four tugs then manoeuvred the flagship into the dry-dock before the canal-lock-type gate was shut so that the 135,000 tons of seawater could be pumped out. It was a delicate operation to balance the ship on blocks in the centre of the dock, but the process was essential if the crew were going to find and repair the leak. A 60-centimetre crack in one of the sea chest welds turned out to be the problem, but it was eventually welded shut.

After nine days in dry-dock, the flood gates were opened and Ark Royal was re-floated. She was then dispatched to rejoin her task group in the North Atlantic. With the volcanic ash cloud having dispersed, flying operations and live firing exercises were also resumed. But the British flagship was running late and would have to make up time if she was going to meet the largest peacetime task force assembled in over a decade in Norfolk, Virginia, the biggest naval base on earth.

With time running out, the ship's route was pushed a little to the north above the Grand Banks and the wreck

of the Titanic. The weather was cold so the ship's crew were on high alert for icebergs drifting south in the Labrador Current. Lieutenant Phil Davis kept a close eye on the ship's radar to watch for the biggest bergs but smaller growlers were difficult to spot so a constant vigil had to be kept ahead.

To save more time on the Atlantic crossing, Ark Royal was refuelled on the open water by the American ship USNS Wally Schirra (named after a NASA astronaut). This complex operation started with a transfer of lines and hoses while the ships maintained a steady 12 knots about a ship's width apart. The refuelling lasted more than two hours, even though the system was pumping 7,000 litres per minute. At the end of the process, having taken on 800 tons of fuel, the rig was detached and the ships were finally free to move away from one another.

Next up for the crew was an aircraft crash and fire drill designed by Damage Control Officer 'Whiskey' Walker. Casualties were dressed with a variety of wounds so that the paramedics felt as if they were treating people with life-threatening injuries. The fire was simulated with smoke machines and the drill was so realistic that many of the crew believed they were facing a real emergency. The team was given a minute to evacuate the affected compartments before they were infused with fire suppressant gases that were harmful to humans. The drill passed off smoothly and the compartment was eventually reclaimed by the crew.

Helicopter winchmen were also expected to perform peacetime heroics, and on Ark Royal they faced a variety of search-and-rescue exercises. Gareth Edwards was dressed in an immersion suit in case he or his partner went overboard, but they were both safely winched up from, and then returned to, the deck of the ship as she pitched by up to four metres in the Atlantic swell.

The following morning, with Captain John Clink at the helm, Ark Royal arrived in Norfolk, a 12-square-mile base accommodating up to 78 ships. Although she was a formidable weapon in her own right, the carrier was dwarfed by the might of the American fleet: USS Enterprise, USS Harry Truman and USS Theodore Roosevelt, each have 1,100-foot (335-metre) flight decks, around twice as long as the one on Ark Royal.

LEFT Paramedic training.

The ship immediately took on 140 American marines and engineers to service a flight of 12 Harriers that would be used in the Capella Strike operation. More American guests were invited for a party in the ship's hangar, with Vice-Admiral Williams, commander of the US Second Fleet, the resident VIP. At nine o'clock the queen's flag was lowered and the party ended so that the ship's complement could prepare for the following day's activity.

The ship left Norfolk at six in the morning so that the Harriers could be embarked early, but the weather had turned against them and Ark Royal had to change course. Despite the poor conditions, the ship's helicopters continued operating even when the cloud base dropped to 100 feet (30 metres). The American jets, on the other hand, needed a cloud base of at least 100 feet (300 metres) before they would be allowed to land on the carrier because it was their first rendezvous with Ark Royal.

RIGHT The ship bears her famous pennant number: R07

BELOW The busy flight deck.

LEFT A crew member shows attention to detail.

The Lynx was the first helicopter to try landing on the deck. The safe parameters were two degrees of pitch and five degrees of roll so the sea conditions played a critical part in operational deployments. The helicopter moved in from the stern using the ship's superstructure as reference. The much larger Merlin – 14 tons as opposed to the Lynx's three – was next to land. It needed higher winds of 35 knots to be able to land safely so Ark Royal's speed was increased.

Despite steaming nearly a hundred miles south by nightfall, the weather hadn't improved and the cloud base hadn't lifted so embarking the Marine Corps Harriers had to wait until the following morning. With the weather finally improving, the US AV-8B Harriers were able to join the ship. They were slightly different from the British GR9 in that they were equipped with long-range radar and a Gatling gun capable of firing 4,000 rounds per minute.

The aircraft were immediately deployed in a training run that involved attacking a dummy target being towed behind the ship. The tiny splash target was rarely hit but the exercise tested precision strikes from dummy bombs and high-powered machinegun rounds. The first attack was from an altitude of 300 feet (750 metres) and a speed of 500 knots, but, despite getting to within 30 feet (10 metres) of the target, it remained intact. The airmen then got a second chance to attack with their Gatling guns.

The pilots dropped to 2,000 feet (600 metres) and fired on the target in 100-round one-and-a-half-second bursts. In times of war, the rounds would be fitted with incendiary heads that can disable tanks. Despite the ferocious power of the Harrier's weapons, the two-square-metre target remained in one piece. With the training runs over for the day, the ship continued south towards the Mayport naval station in Florida.

Then it was time for Lieutenant Ralph Wood, a British airman on a three-year tour with the American 542 Marine Attack Squadron, to earn his carrier landing qualifications. This required Wood to spend three hours in the jet and make eight landings. Unlike the US carriers, which use a catapult launching system, Ark Royal had a ski jump ramp to help get the Harriers airborne.

While he may have been on his own

in the cockpit, Wood's every move was scrutinised by a team in the flight control tower. His assessors were highly qualified pilots who had served on several tours in war zones. Before Lieutenant Wood was allowed to land, he had to complete two 600 mile-per-hour circuits of the ship. He then had to bring his aircraft to a hover above the ship while it was underway at 28 knots. (Having earned their qualifications, Harrier pilots were reassessed every six months to ensure they were always combat ready.) Any mistakes at this late stage might cost the pilot his flight status, but his landings were competent and he passed the final test.

The following day was declared a no-fly day so the ship headed for open water and clear airspace to conduct a live weapons test. A large inflatable red balloon was deployed by one of the support ships so Ark Royal could engage the so-called tomato with her 20-millimetre cannon, forward mini-gun and forward general purpose machinegun (GPMG). The ship's seven GPMGs were accurate to 6,000 feet (1,800 metres), the mini-guns fired 800 rounds per minute and could shred an enemy aircraft in flight, and the two cannon had explosive rounds and a range of up to seven kilometres.

The guided-missile destroyer USS Barry towed the tomato three kilometres behind the carrier and gave Ark Royal 10 minutes in which to sink it. The 20mm cannon and mini-gun both jammed during the exercise but the crew quickly cleared the blockages as they would in a combat situation. The tomato took a few hits but was easily repaired in time for the next exercise.

With the American Harrier pilots about to disembark, Ark Royal's crew spotted a chance to make some money for their welfare fund by selling T-shirts, mugs, coins and other mementos. On their last night onboard, the British threw their visitors a party on the quarterdeck.

Junior navigator Sub-Lieutenant Ed Rees was not at the party because he was preparing to pilot the ship into Mayport. Although the captain would take control and berth the ship once inside the harbour, Rees needed to navigate the tight entrance and dangerous shallows on the last stretch, as well as taking into account the strong tidal stream. It took him most of the night to calculate safe passage into the anchorage.

The following morning, the US Harriers took off for the last time and headed for their bases on the mainland. Ark Royal then made her way tentatively into the port under Captain Clink, and the crew enjoyed six days' leave in glorious sunshine. As four other ships from the Auriga Task Force were also in Mayport, physical training instructor Steve Losh decided to organise an inter-ship sports event including rugby, football and volleyball.

Shore leave gave the ship's company the chance to relax and enjoy themselves, and the beer flowed freely at the sports event (won by Ark Royal's crew). Some of the ship's company stayed onboard, however, and were put through drills by Warrant Officer Simon Cox. With Ark Royal about to sail for a royal engagement in Canada, it was important that the 96 sailors not on shore leave were ready to be presented to the queen.

Her six days in the sun over, Ark Royal left Mayport and headed north back to Norfolk naval base in Virginia. On leaving the port, an attack from fast pirate boats was simulated so the entire crew was at actions stations. In 2000, 17 sailors had been killed on the destroyer USS Cole in the Yemeni port of Aden by a suicide team piloting a small boat packed with explosives, so the carrier's crew had to be prepared to counter such a threat.

If repeated attempts to contact the two boats had been ignored, Ark Royal would have been forced to fire warning shots across their bows. The two vessels backed off in the simulation but, had they been real pirates or terrorists and kept on approaching, the ship's crew would have fired on them.

The kitchen had to remain open when the ship was at action stations but the menu was limited to pasta Bolognese and a single vegetarian option.

The entire ship's company had to be in and out in 45 minutes and still leave time for the galley to be cleaned, so 1,000 people could only be fed if it was a slick operation. The food during action messing had to be at 75°C so it didn't take more than a few minutes to eat. The crew then simply disposed of their paper plates and returned to their stations immediately.

Ark Royal then headed for Halifax, Nova Scotia, on Canada's eastern seaboard. There she collected six British GR9 Harriers of the Royal Air Force's

LEFT View of *Ark Royal* from one of her helicopters.

One Squadron that would stay with the ship for the next two months. The GR9 carried sidewinder missiles or up to six laser-guided bombs so it was a formidable weapon in its own right. The Harriers had previously been on an eight-week tour to Afghanistan and would now be flying reconnaissance, air-to-air combat and bombing missions in the North Atlantic. It still wasn't known aboard ship, however, that this would be their last official deployment.

Their first war game involved carrying a 1,000lb bomb to the Oceania airbase in West Virginia. This was an extremely delicate mission for the pilots as the bombs were live and had to be dropped with pinpoint accuracy to avoid inflicting casualties on their own men on the ground. Ark Royal's ordnance was stored well below the waterline, but the bombs were eventually winched into position. Their detonators, fusing

BELOW *Ark Royal* is helped into port by a tug and harbour pilot.

units and guidance systems were added in a sealed chamber on the flight deck at the last minute. The bombs were then winched up to the flight deck and secured to the aircraft.

Pilot Nick Lane used his heads-up display to get a fix on the target and make his final approach. The 1,000lb bomb he dropped on the base was typical of the ordnance used against small buildings and other structures in war zones like Afghanistan, and it had an effective blast range of about 100 feet (30 metres). His bomb landed just 20 feet (six metres) from the target. Then, with their fuel running out, the Harriers returned to the flagship.

The following day another exercise simulated a missile attack on the fleet, with the Type 42 Destroyer HMS Liverpool the target. Smoke machines were used to add realism to the exercise and hamper the rescue effort. To create a little more confusion, a flood was triggered in the ship's engine room. Everyone onboard was trained to deal with minor flooding but it still divided resources by drawing damage control personnel away from the fire. Soft wooden wedges were hammered into the hole to slow the incoming water.

ABOVE Bombs being transferred by winch.

They absorbed the liquid quickly and then expanded to fill the hole and seal the breach in the hull.

HMS Liverpool's engines were then shut down and her power was cut, further hampering the teams battling to save her. Fire-fighting and damage control units now had to work in the dark. With the ship drifting, she was at

RIGHT Crew
members proudly line
the deck.

the mercy of the currents and an unseen enemy. It was time for Ark Royal to spring into action.

Supplies to repair the breach completely were ferried across by rigid inflatable boat, by which time the flagship was close enough to pass tow lines between the vessels. The lines got heavier and heavier until the thick cable was capable of withstanding the strain between the ships. If the line were to part under the stress, it had enough power to kill as well as breach the hull. For this reason, Captain Clink called a halt to the exercise when the cable drew taut because it was too dangerous to complete the mission without it being a genuine emergency.

As the ships approached Halifax, the weather closed in. Fog is one of the most dangerous conditions a ship can encounter: the passenger liner Empress of Ireland was lost with 1,012 people in the St Lawrence Seaway when she collided with a Norwegian collier, the SS Storstad, in dense fog in May 1914; and the Italian liner Andrea Doria sank after hitting the MS Stockholm in poor visibility in 1956.

Ark Royal was also on high alert because of the number of small fishing vessels in the area. She then received a mayday from one of them. On receiving a distress call, all ships in the area must acknowledge the signal and assist if possible. The crew of the Merlin helicopter were given a brief meteorological report so they knew what to expect if they were dispatched to the scene.

Initial reports suggested the other vessel was on fire, but a second report stated that a man had made it onto an upturned life-raft. As the Merlin was readied for launch, another message from the coastguard informed them that the man had been recovered and they could stand down.

With the weather deteriorating again, the harbour pilot was dispatched to Ark Royal to guide her into Halifax. Visibility dropped to just 300 feet (100 metres) as she entered the harbour but the ship's company was still required to line her decks. A 21-gun salute let everyone know that the flagship was finally in port.

Steve Losh couldn't have his crew getting restless straight away so he organised a boxing tournament in the ship's hangar. The only difference between this and a regular fight night was that the boxers would be blindfolded. They

had little rattles in their hands so they could find and fight each other by ear. Referee Matt Short ended up taking a pasting but the ship's crew, most of whom were in drag, lapped up the entertainment.

The ship's company then spent the following morning working off their hangovers to prepare for a visit by David Cameron. It required a huge effort to make the ship presentable for such a high-ranking VIP. It was the prime minister's first visit to a warship on active duty and he was suitably impressed with Ark Royal. His speech to the crew, however, gave no hint that the ship was about to be decommissioned.

As part of the Canadian bicentennial celebrations, Ark Royal was one of 27 vessels from eight countries that lined up outside the port to be reviewed by Queen Elizabeth II. The fog took a while to lift so Captain Clink decided to wait before moving out to their new anchorage. The ship almost didn't make

RIGHT A V-22 Osprey on display at the American Helicopter Museum & Education Center.

it out of port at all as the crane operator needed to remove the gangplank didn't turn up for work. It was an irritating delay for Clink and the 1,000 sailors under his command.

When the ship eventually got under-way, the thick fog hampered their pro-gress but, once in position, her one-ton anchors were released from the fore-castle. When a ship anchors in fog, it is important, even with all the radar and satellite technologies that exist today, to ring a bell warning other ships of their presence and position.

As the fog finally lifted, the ship's crew lined up on deck for the review. The queen boarded the Canadian ship St John and headed out towards the fleet. She was given three cheers as she passed Ark Royal and inspected the remaining vessels in the fleet. With the formalities over, the carrier left port and headed for clearer skies out in the Atlantic. The queen was so impressed with the dis-play that she left instructions to splice the mainbrace, an order for the ship's company to be allowed a large measure of rum. It is a popular tradition with the crew for obvious reasons.

The next morning an unusual air-craft, an American Osprey V-22, was

welcomed onto the flagship. The plane takes off vertically like a helicopter but then rotates its huge nine-metre rotors forward and uses its wings to fly like a conventional fixed-wing aircraft. The Osprey had arrived to pick up American

ABOVE Crew members wait patiently to disembark.

THE FINAL VOYAGE

RIGHT Making
steady progress.

naval personnel who had been meeting Captain Clink to discuss further fleet operations.

Ark Royal would now be at sea for the next month as she prepared for a huge operation with the US and Canadian fleets to fend off simulated attacks from small gunboats. In times of war, or when threats were detected, Ark Royal immediately launched its early warning system. The airborne surveillance and control (ASaC) Sea King helicopter carried such sophisticated radar that it could track up to 400 targets simultaneously, some as small as a bicycle, over a hundred miles away.

The ASaC crew soon picked up an unknown contact approaching the task group. Although the Sea King wasn't armed, it called Ark Royal for a smaller, faster Westland Lynx to lend support. The Lynx is one of the most agile combat helicopters in the world and is equipped with a variety of weapons, such as M3M cannon or air-to-ground missiles.

The target was soon identified as a speedboat closing on the task force at 35 knots. This time it was being controlled remotely but in a war zone it could be loaded with explosives or crewed

by Somali pirates. Ark Royal put up a defensive shield of firepower from the 20mm cannon, the mini-guns and the GPMGs. Although it was difficult to hit at range, it could not escape from the Lynx even by turning and trying to escape, and the helicopter's gun crew destroyed the enemy vessel within seconds.

Having dealt with this simulated threat, Ark Royal then faced a real emergency when water started flooding one of her lower compartments. This was an extremely serious situation. Even a small amount of water entering a ship can have catastrophic consequences. In 1987, the car ferry Herald of Free Enterprise rolled over and sank off the port of Zeebrugge, with the loss of 193 lives, when water entered her car deck via an open bow door.

Water in the flooded compartment soon reached live electrical equipment making the diagnosis even more hazardous. Damage control specialist 'Whiskey' Walker had to call for the power supply to be switched off before anyone could enter the hold to pump out the water. He soon discovered that the water was actually an overflow from the ship's freshwater tanks and not

THE FINAL VOYAGE

RIGHT There's not much room to manoeuvre on the busy flight deck.

seawater as was originally feared. With the source of the leak identified, the crew were able to seal it quickly.

With everything back under control, the Merlin crew practised search and rescue operations on the open ocean using a dummy. The pilot couldn't see the target so had to rely on instructions from an observer in the helicopter's belly to locate it with the grappling hook.

The next air defence exercise was a carrier versus Harrier duel that was designed to put both through their paces. Flown by Lieutenant Commander Matt Devin, the Harrier was taken out to a 100 miles before returning at 100 feet (30 metres) to try to avoid the carrier's early warning systems. The carrier had two options: shoot the aircraft down or avoid its missiles by outmanoeuvring the jet. For a 21,000-ton ship, Ark Royal was surprisingly agile and, with her array of defences, she had a nasty bite. Devin knew that the carrier's flight deck was her most important asset – destroy that and the carrier loses its main advantage and can't launch any aircraft.

Devin flew in low and fast and deployed his countermeasures but the carrier had already turned hard to starboard to bring her mini-guns online. A second sharp turn to port gave the gun crews another shot at the Harrier. But the exercise was eventually scored as a victory for Devin. He executed a steep climb and then dived out of the sun to launch his missiles, but the crew on Ark Royal's bridge didn't see him until it was too late.

These smaller exercises were building up to the main event, a four-week war game against the US mainland under the command of Commodore Simon Ancona. The eight-ship British task group would approach the coast and disgorge a marine amphibious landing unit to take strategic enemy positions onshore so that humanitarian aid could then be delivered. The US navy would provide stern opposition.

HMS Sutherland was sent ahead to patrol for enemy ships and submarines. Her crew immediately spotted a suspicious vessel, so the ship was sent to intercept it before it could get near Ark Royal. The American warship was posing as a trawler from a hostile rogue state so the Sutherland had to deal with this threat by sending across an armed boarding party to inspect the ship.

The American naval personnel slipped into character while the boarding party searched the ship. The trawler's crew suddenly turned on the British sailors and the situation became tense, although it was eventually resolved. Even though the scenario wasn't real, the teams on both sides treated it as they would in a combat zone. Practising for every eventuality saves lives should the crew face real pirates or other unknown vessels in the future.

No sooner had the exercise finished than Ark Royal ran into difficulty. One of the four gas turbines that powered her had malfunctioned. The trouble was traced to debris in the oil system that lubricated the turbine. If the problem had continued unchecked, the engine could have failed catastrophically and shattered the turbine blades. Repairing the engine was a top priority because if the ship couldn't generate enough headwind, the Harriers wouldn't be able to take off. Being denied air support in a war zone could compromise

BELOW Harriers ready for take-off.

the entire task group, so time was of the essence. Thankfully, the ship carried two spare engines, so the defective one could be replaced.

The faulty Rolls-Royce Olympus was removed and placed in a lift that took it up to the main hangar, and the new engine was installed in a delicate five-hour operation. It was then gradually brought up to speed to test it was operational. With the ship back on schedule, it was time to begin the amphibious assault on the American coast.

The area, codenamed Amberland, is a 650-square-kilometre marine corps training area and naval base called Camp Lejeune that also has 22 kilometres of beaches. It was the perfect place for Commodore Ancona to launch an assault by land, air and sea. The assault itself was spearheaded by HMS Albion, the command platform for the amphibious task group that doubled as a landing dock. On the ship's vehicle deck, Royal Marines from 42 Commando prepared their equipment for a full-scale beach landing. Each of their four landing craft could carry 70 tons of hardware for the assault. The ship's well dock was then flooded so the landing craft could be floated off her stern.

Air support would be provided by Ark Royal, which maintained her position 90 kilometres offshore. However, both the carrier's Sea Kings were out of action so the flagship's long-range surveillance capability was severely compromised. Parts from one were cannibalised to make repairs to the other's engine fire extinguisher so that it could be in the air by the time the jets took off.

ABOVE An old Rolls-Royce Olympus turbojet on display at the Fleet Air Arm Museum, RNAS Yeovilton.

The Sea King was eventually launched in time to support the jets and provide long-range radar coverage. (The Lynx was already airborne as a gun platform.) And the Harriers were standing by to destroy any targets deemed a threat by the marines on the ground. Those marines were then put through their paces in a variety of landing craft, from hovercraft to inflatable boats to small amphibious craft, to test their readiness to face hostile troops on the beaches.

Having successfully completed their mission to deliver humanitarian aid into hostile territory, the marines retreated to their landing craft for the return trip to HMS Albion.

The weather had turned, however, and the landing craft found it difficult to negotiate a rising sea. Ark Royal's rescue helicopters were 45 minutes away and the Albion couldn't move with her dock still flooded so the landing craft, which was now taking on water, had to make its own way through the heavy swell. The marines had to bail with buckets but they eventually reached the mother ship.

With the lander safely back onboard, Ark Royal dispatched her jets to shoot down hostile F-18s that were threatening the task group. One of the Harriers developed an electrical fault in flight, however, and had to divert to the naval air base at Oceania in Virginia. Flight Lieutenant Martin Pert was engaging the enemy aircraft in a dogfight when his computers malfunctioned and his radios cut out. He decided that it was too risky to attempt a landing on Ark Royal with most of his systems down so he diverted to the naval base instead. The carrier's engineering team were dispatched to change the faulty part but it wasn't a quick fix and Pert was stranded for two days before he could rejoin the squadron aboard ship.

Meanwhile, there was an equally serious incident involving one of HMS Ocean's Sea King helicopters. She had developed an oil contamination problem that could disable her tail rotor so Lieutenant Ian Pearson requested an immediate landing.

The mother ship and the US mainland were too far away so the only option was to land on Ark Royal. The ship's ground crew only had a minute to clear the deck but Pearson landed safely. The problem was traced to a wearing gearbox, which needed to be replaced.

Although the war game against

the Americans was in full swing, an announcement from back home was about to change the lives of everyone onboard. Under the proposed defence cuts, Ark Royal was going to be decommissioned and scrapped. This was a big blow to morale and the crew were visibly upset. Despite the bad news, they had to remain on high alert for the rest of the ship's operational life. Indeed, they had to rehearse for an immediate attack by hostile aircraft in the tropical

heat off Florida. The entire crew were dressed in their fire suits to prepare for missile strikes. Smoke machines were again used to simulate the effects of several missiles hitting the superstructure.

'Whiskey' Walker was called in to assess the damage and evacuate personnel from the bridge. With everyone on the roof of the bridge, it appeared that the ship would be at the mercy of the enemy aircraft, but Ark Royal's designers had planned for the worst. The ship

BELOW Crew take part in the fire-fighting module.

could still be piloted if communications were patched up from the captain in the operations room below to Commander Bellfield on the roof.

With the crisis deepening, Walker organised a command huddle for vital personnel in the command bunker or HQ1. The fire was spreading quickly through the ship, however, and it soon breached HQ1 so the team had to evacuate and reconvene in their back-up location, HQ2. Their troubles weren't over yet: the fire had also entered the officers' mess and knocked out the ship's ventilation system. With temperatures approaching 50°C, the fire-fighting teams were now hampered by their protective gear and several were overheating. Walker had to evacuate anyone suffering from heat stress before the fires could be attacked.

During all the confusion a real distress message was broadcast over the ship's public address system. Walker was again dispatched to assess the situation. Two sailors were suffering with heat exhaustion because they hadn't been rotated during the fire-fighting module. It was time to end the exercise before it caused more casualties.

On the way back across the Atlantic, the Harriers of One Squadron were recalled to RAF Cottesmore in the UK. As the last GR9 took to the air off the ski jump, fixed-wing aircraft operations on the fleet's flagship came to an end.

Despite returning home to be decommissioned, Ark Royal's crew were still put through their paces with a man overboard drill. A dummy was thrown over the side and the ship had to make an immediate emergency stop. In near-freezing water, human life expectancy is measured in minutes. The dummy had to be back onboard within 12 to satisfy naval requirements so a rigid-hulled inflatable boat was launched to recover it. By now, the rescue team only had eight minutes left.

A person in the water can easily become obscured by small swells so the crew on the carrier had to direct the rescue boat towards the casualty. With three minutes left, the body was found and retrieved. The team then raced back to the carrier. They beat the clock by 30 seconds and rushed the dummy in for a medical examination and resuscitation.

The following day, a Sunday, the ship's bishop, Reverend Richard Ellingham, held his usual church service, his last on Ark Royal. No sooner was it over than the ship faced a simulated biological weapons attack. 'Whiskey' Walker ordered all the ship's airtight doors closed so that filtered, pressurised air could be pumped into her three main citadels: forward, mid-ship and aft. With the air pressure raised inside the ship, if there were any leaks, air could only escape and poisonous substances couldn't enter.

As soon as the ship was locked down, the pressurisation process began. Each citadel reported pressure readings back to HQ1 so progress could be monitored. Walker then checked for leaks around the hatches. He moved between citadels by passing through airlocks but some of the crew weren't as careful and the pressure suddenly collapsed. If it had been a real-world scenario, the biological agent could have entered the ship and disabled her crew.

If Ark Royal had become contaminated during a chemical, nuclear or biological attack, the ship itself would remain contaminated even after it had cleared the danger area. Walker therefore supervised the pumping of millions of litres of salt water across every inch of her exterior, particularly the flight deck. The ship was then put into a forced roll to ensure any remaining contaminants were washed over the side.

As the ship neared the UK, the helicopters from HMS Ocean that had hitched a ride were finally able to depart for Yeovilton naval air station in Somerset. They would be the last aircraft to leave the flagship. The carrier then anchored just outside Portsmouth while Captain Clink waited for clearance to enter the harbour. As it was his last deployment, he asked for permission to bring his wife and children onboard. The crew then lined the decks as Ark Royal finally made port to an emotional welcome from family and friends.

In October 2010, the ship was in Portsmouth to take on new captain, Jerry Kyd, a man who had previously served onboard as a midshipman. The defence review may have signed her death warrant but Ark Royal still needed a crew for her final journey, although they were still smarting from what they saw as a knife in the back. A few months earlier the prime minister had tried to reassure them that the ship had a place in the navy, but as soon as she returned home she was being decommissioned, with at least five thousand redundancies. It was a bitter blow to morale.

The ship was sent on a farewell tour to Scotland, Newcastle and Hamburg before returning to Portsmouth. The carrier, however, still had time to run helicopter training exercises from her flight deck. A Merlin carried out a dangerous mid-air refuelling operation while hovering above a ship maintaining 22 knots. The exercise was designed to test the crews in case they couldn't land and, after 15 minutes, they'd taken on two tons of fuel.

With the helicopter out of the way, it was time to begin removing the ship's armament. Her Sidewinder and Maverick missiles, bombs, rockets, torpedoes and other ordnance were transferred to the main hangar. When the ship reached Scotland, the ammunition was offloaded over three days and transferred to a secret military location in the Highlands. With 25 tons of high explosives onboard, the greatest fear during this delicate operation was fire, so the crew ran several emergency drills.

Warrant Officer 'Whiskey' Walker oversaw the exercises even though he was supposed to have retired from the navy when they reached Portsmouth. He designated two of the crew to receive serious burn injuries and then triggered the fire. All personnel had to report to their emergency stations, which was the precursor to the 'abandon ship' order.

No sooner had the drill finished than a real emergency came to the crew's attention. Water was flooding into the ship and about to enter the female ratings' mess. Walker traced the source of the leak to an unsecured waste disposal pipe beneath one of the bathrooms and radioed the information back to HQ1 so the team could make a decision on how to tackle the flooding.

The damage control team decided that the flooding could only be contained by deliberately listing the ship. HQ1 ordered Ark Royal to steer in a slow circle so the water could be bailed before it reached the dental surgery and the women's compartment. As the water was contaminated, the decks had to be washed down with powerful cleaning

agents before the incident could be declared over.

The ship soon entered Loch Long on the northwest coast of Scotland and headed for the Glen Mallan jetty. Once there, her munitions could be safely offloaded before being taken to the Glen Douglas Depot. Forty tons of munitions were transferred to the flight deck but two Maverick missile boxes had not been properly secured so they were taken back down to the hangar to be checked.

Petty Officer Mark Brown scrutinised the missile itself to make sure it hadn't been damaged or tampered with. Both missiles were soon declared safe and they were then taken off with the 1,000lb bombs. The rest of the ordnance had to wait until the following morning.

That evening, Captain Kyd welcomed a special guest onboard. Jock Moffat served on the third incarnation of Ark Royal as a Swordfish pilot during the Second World War. In 1941 he was one of the men who flew operations against the mighty German battleship Bismarck, so he was an A-list celebrity in naval terms. Indeed it was Jock's torpedo that damaged Bismarck's rudder and effectively ended the contest.

THE FINAL VOYAGE

RIGHT Royal Marines Band.

Unable to steer, the British fleet closed in and finished her off in what was one of the greatest naval engagements of the war.

In the hangar the following day, Lieutenant Vicky Shervill continued offloading the ship's ammunition, including 136 bombs. It took another two days to empty her magazines, by which time the tiger had officially lost her teeth and become just another ship rather than a warship. With this phase of the operation complete, Ark Royal headed for the port where she'd been built and launched in 1981: Newcastle. On the way, she picked up four Harriers from One Squadron so the ship had aircraft onboard when she was opened to the public. Over the next two days, 10,000 people said their goodbyes to the pride of the British fleet.

The ship's final trip abroad took her across the North Sea to Hamburg. On the way, the Harriers left the flight deck via the ski jump for the last time. The

RIGHT Royal Marines Band.

new Queen Elizabeth-class carriers with their F-35 aircraft wouldn't come into service for another decade, so there'd be a considerable period when Britain had no naval air defences.

hand over the flagship status to HMS Albion. The weather was poor and the flight deck was soon covered in snow, which put the embarkation of her helicopters in doubt. But the crew rallied one last time to clear the decks and welcome the Sea Kings. (The helicopters were also being decommissioned in line with the strategic defence spending review.) Although Lynx helicopters were also supposed to be joining them, thick fog prevented them from landing and the ship entered Portsmouth without them.

The ship's company lined up on her flight deck in Procedure Alpha to salute the people of Portsmouth who'd

When the ship reached the German port, the crew had their final shore leave. It was a chance to let their hair down and toast the Mighty Ark. The ship then returned to Portsmouth to turned out to welcome them home for the last time. It was now time for the Sea Kings to disembark. Ark Royal had made her final journey and would now be scrapped.

Chapter 7

The Future

BELOW Geoffrey
Hoon (right) in a
press conference with
Donald H. Rumsfeld
(left) at the Pentagon
in 2003.

It seems unlikely at the moment that the Ark Royal name will live on in the next generation of navy warships. In 1997, the new labour government's strategic defence review recommended that when the Invincible-class carriers had reached the end of their service life they should be replaced with two large aircraft carriers in the order of 40,000 tons. Two years later, six companies were asked to tender for the assessment phase, and the Ministry of Defence eventually asked BAE Systems and the Thales Group to submit designs.

In 2001, the UK signed up to the USA's Joint Strike Fighter programme that enabled them to bid for the Lockheed Martin F-35, which could be adapted for carrier use. As they were expected to be in service for half a century, however, the ships would have to be future-proofed so that they could accommodate a variety of helicopters and other aircraft. In 2003, Defence Secretary Geoff Hoon announced that the Thales Group had won the £3.9 billion contract to design the ships, but

BELOW Geoffrey Hoon (right) in a press conference with Donald H. Rumsfeld (left) at the Pentagon in 2003.

that BAE Systems would also be involved as a contractor. These contracts were eventually signed in 2008, and Babcock Marine in Rosyth and Cammell Laird in Birkenhead were given the go-ahead to start work on the two ships.

Eighty thousand tons of steel was ordered from the Corus Group, £3 million was spent on fibre-optic communications, £1 million was spent on desalination systems to provide the 500 tons of freshwater the ships would need each day, and the £13 million contract for the aircraft lifts was awarded to MacTaggart Scott. A joint venture between BAE Systems and the VT Group, known initially as the BVT Surface Fleet and subsequently as BAE Systems Surface Ships, then signed up to fulfilling forty percent of the construction phase.

Having awarded more lucrative contracts for the weapon handling systems, air traffic control software, pumps and engineering products, emergency diesel generators, gas turbines, generators,

ABOVE The cockpit and instrument panel of a Lockheed-Martin F-35 Lightning II at the Canada Aviation & Space Museum.

propellers and shafts, and steering gear and stabilisers, the first cut of steel for the Queen Elizabeth was made in July 2009 (work began on the second carrier in May 2011). Six shipyards around the British Isles would build various blocks before they would be transported via ocean-going barge to be assembled at

Rosyth in Scotland. The overall construction programme involves 10,000 personnel from nearly 100 companies.

Her command system has three main functions: the information system uses existing computer hardware, internal networks and C41 software to control the carrier; a communication control management system allows the ship to be configured for internal and external communications; and the air management and protection system runs the ship's new highly mechanised weapons handling systems and manages her airborne strike group.

HMS Queen Elizabeth is expected to enter service in 2016, with her sister, HMS Prince of Wales, following two years later. They will displace 65,000 tons (three times larger than Ark Royal) and will be 920 feet long, the largest ships ever built for the Royal Navy. Two Rolls-Royce Marine Trent gas turbines will provide 100,000 shaft horsepower, while four Wärtsilä diesel generators will deliver another 54,000 horsepower

RIGHT An F-35B Lighting II.

to twin screws weighing 33 tons each. They will give the ships a top speed of around 25 knots and, with a full fuel load of 8,600 tons, they'll have a range of 10,000 miles. (This power would be enough to supply a town the size of Swindon.) Due to budgetary limitations and concern over the final displacement, the carriers will forgo side armour and reinforced bulkheads. They will each be covered in 370 acres of paint, enough to coat Hyde Park.

The flight deck will have an equivalent area of three football pitches but will have two towers instead of the usual one. The aft tower will be used to control flight operations, while the forward superstructure will house the bridge and will be used to control the ship. There are several advantages of using this configuration: the area of the flight deck can be increased; turbulence opposite the main command and control centre will be reduced; and the space below-decks can be

ABOVE Cinema for relaxation.

better allocated.

There will be a further nine decks beneath the flight deck, with the main 155-metre hangar being able to accommodate at least 20 fixed- and rotary-wing aircraft. Two hydraulic lifts will be capable of transferring four F-35s to the flight deck in under a minute.

The ships' 680 regular crew and 1,000 fleet air arm contingent will be catered for in four galleys and the same number of dining areas. There will be a cinema and gym for relaxation, and a medical centre to treat illness and injury.

The two carriers will use the S1850M long-range radar – which is capable

RIGHT A Close-In Weapon System (CIWS) fires during a systems test.

of tracking up to 1,000 targets over 250 miles away – and the BAE Artisan maritime radar for mid to short range and navigation. The latter system is so sensitive that it can pick out an object the size of a tennis ball at 12 miles. They will also be heavily defended with the Phalanx Close-in Weapons System (CIWS), and radar-guided 20-millimetre Gatling guns to defend against anti-ship missiles. They will also be equipped with DS30M guns capable of taking out fast attack boats that may be armed with short-range missiles, rocket-propelled grenades or explosives. The ships' last line of defence are their mini-guns, six-barrelled machineguns capable of firing 6,000 rounds per minute at incoming aircraft or gunboats.

The carriers are also formidable offensive weapons: they will each host a minimum of 12 and a maximum of 36 F-35 Lightning II fixed wing fighter-bombers, although the squadron will not become fully operational on the ships until 2020. The navy is still unsure which configuration it will use but will either go with the catapult launch and arrestor recovery system used by the F-35C or the ski-jump take-off and vertical landing F-35B. Either way, the

ship will be able to launch 24 aircraft in 15 minutes and recover them at a rate of one every minute. If the vertical landing configuration is selected, the bow will be have to be inclined by 13° ¬– it seems likely that a steam catapult or electromagnetic launch system will be retrofitted at some point in the future and the design teams have allowed for this. The deck will have three runways so launch and recovery operations can proceed simultaneously. Blast deflectors will also be fitted, and two vertical landing pads will be positioned near the stern.

If all 36 aircraft are posted to the ships, they will only be able to carry four helicopters. If not all the F-35s are in service, and depending on the mission, up to 12 Chinooks and eight Apaches could also be deployed, although the navy is likely to insist on continuing the tradition of using the Merlin / Lynx combination.

Two variants of the AugustaWestland Merlin helicopter will serve on the ships. They both use the same engine configuration and airframe powered by three Rolls-Royce Turbomecas and have an extended range of around 1,000 miles. The first variant can carry 38

troops or 16 stretchers, the second a dedicated anti-submarine electronic warfare suite and advanced sonar systems. Depending on the mission, the helicopters will be equipped with anti-ship and other air-to-ground or air-to-air missiles, rockets, torpedoes and up to three machineguns.

A second helicopter, the Lynx Wildcat, will enter service in 2015. It also boasts an electronic warfare suite with active dipping sonar, long-range radar, electro-optical imaging and covert surveillance programmes, as well as electronic countermeasures for defence. It can be armed with missiles, torpedoes, depth charges and heavy machineguns, and has an effective range of 600 miles.

The Invincible-class carriers, of which Ark Royal was one, relied upon Sea King helicopters for early warning and control. The two new ships may continue the tradition for their Maritime Airborne Surveillance and Control (MASC) programme, although there are other options: Lockheed Martin could supply a converted Merlin for the role; AugustaWestland could deliver a dedicated Sea King; the American tilt-rotor Bell V-22 Osprey could be used; or, providing the catapult launch system is installed, the twin-turboprop Grumman E-2 Hawkeye aircraft could be brought into service. The latter option has the most powerful radar and boasts a greater speed and range than any

BELOW American tilt-rotor Bell V-22 Osprey.

of the helicopters, and it would also secure approval from the French and American navies.

Although plans for the two ships will no doubt be revised over the coming years, it seems unlikely that either, despite vociferous support for continuing the tradition, will be renamed at this late stage. So, for the foreseeable future, there will be no vessel in the navy bearing the name of its most famous ship. However, it seems inconceivable that there will never be another Ark Royal. In a world with an uncertain future, ships of the line will always be needed to patrol international waters, protect nations and go to war to bring about peace, and another Ark Royal is sure to play a part in the Royal Navy of the future.

Design & Artwork: ALEX YOUNG

Published by: DEMAND MEDIA LIMITED & G2 ENTERTAINMENT LIMITED

Publishers: JASON FENWICK & JULES GAMMOND

Written by: LIAM MCCANN